ALL ASHLAR STONEWORK TO BE ...
...R WEATHERED. RUBBLE WALL TO BE PO...
...BE KEPT BACK AT LEAST 1" FRO... ...W.
... IN AS LONG LAMINATIONS AS POSSIBLE ...A
...LE DOWN THE FACE OF THE WALL, OR TO REME... A
...TIONS 6 TO 1.   GATE TO BE STANDARD TYPE "E" SEE STANDARD

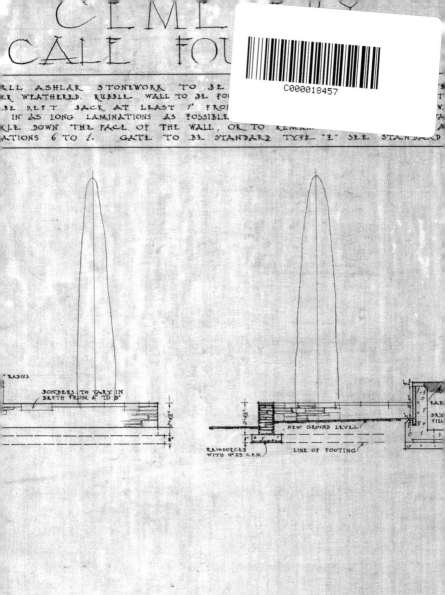

" RADIUS

BONDERS TO VARY IN
DEPTH FROM 6" TO 9"

NEW GROUND LEVEL

REINFORCE
WITH N° 23 R.E.M.   LINE OF FOOTING

BONDER 6" DEEP.

Epitaphs of the Great War: The Somme

Epitaphs of the Great War: The Somme

SARAH WEARNE

UNIFORM

1916
2016

UNIFORM

Uniform
an imprint of Unicorn Publishing Group

Unicorn Publishing Group
101 Wardour Street
London W1F 0UG
www.unicornpublishing.org

First published by Uniform 2016
© Sarah Wearne 2016, © Unicorn Publishing Group, 2016

A CIP catalogue record for this book is available
from the British Library

ISBN 978-1-910500-521

Printed and bound in Czech Republic

Photographs on pages: 6, 17, 42, 51, 53, 57, 67, 73, 75, 84/5,
95, 101, 117, 121, 126/7 © James Kerr

Photographs on pages 11, 110 © Sarah Wearne

Acknowledgements

I should like to thank James Kerr for permission to use some of the beautiful photographs he took of the battlefield cemeteries for his book *Silent Landscapes*, Doughty and Kerr 2016. I should also like to thank my son, Harry Wearne, for building and supporting the website www.epitaphsofthegreatwar.com and its associated Twitter account, @WWInscriptions, on which this book is based. This project would have been impossible without him. And finally, my very grateful thanks to Ryan Gearing of Unicorn Publishing Group who began following me on Twitter and then suggested that the project might make a good book – with his help I hope it has. I said 'finally' but really feel that my final thanks should be to my husband for his support over many, many years, and to all the members of my family who have lived the First World War for most of their lives.

Devonshire
Cemetery

PREFACE

Of all the voices of the First World War there is one that has been consistently overlooked, the voice of the bereaved. And yet it has been there, hiding in plain sight, for almost a hundred years. Walk through any Commonwealth War Graves Commission cemetery and the brief inscriptions at the base of the headstones, masterpieces of compact emotion, will speak to you of love, joy, grief and pride, hope and despair. They will tell you where the soldiers came from, who their parents were, how they died, what they looked like, where they went to school what their job was. They will outline the cause for which they died – and they will even question it. They will quote the Bible and Shakespeare, Tennyson and Rupert Brooke, hymns and popular songs and in so doing reveal the cultural references of the era and the values of the society in which they lived.

These inscriptions have a strange genesis. It had never occurred to the bereaved that dead soldiers belonged to the State. Whilst the war was in progress they could understand the ban on the repatriation of bodies but when this was confirmed as policy after the Armistice there was an outcry. And not only were families not going to be allowed to bring their dead home but they weren't going to be allowed to choose their own headstones. The State, in the form of the Imperial War Graves Commission, had decided on a uniform shape and design for everyone, a curve-topped, rectangular stone not even a cross. To many families this was a second, bitter bereavement forcing some of them to question what freedom they had all been fighting for if they were now going to have to 'submit to the tyranny of the State'. As the mother of three dead sons put it, 'never before in the history of man has a parent or widow been deprived of their right to erect a personal memorial'.

But the Commission was determined that the cemeteries should 'speak in one voice of one death, one sacrifice, endured by Britain for the freedom of nations and the freedom of man'. They argued that to allow the families any choice over the style of headstone would destroy the cemeteries as a visual symbol of a great army that had fought together and died together in one common cause. Worse, it would destroy the outward and visible sign of the fact that in the eyes of the State all the deaths were equal whether the casualty was a general or a private, the son of a marquis or of a washerwoman. The Commission was intransigent.

However, it was this intransigence that ultimately enabled these cemeteries to articulate the greatest individuality of any buried army in history. The decision to have a headstone meant that there was room for an inscription. This would allow the Roman Catholic community, who were agitating because they feared their relations might not have received the Last Rites before they died, to remedy this with a formulaic text or prayer such as: 'O sacred heart of Jesus have mercy on his soul' or, 'Immaculate heart of Mary intercede for him. Jesus have mercy on him'. Such formulas were designed to ease the dead man's path through purgatory.

And if this concession was to be made for the Roman Catholic community it should be allowed for everyone. The Commission therefore announced that next-of-kin would be allowed to choose a headstone inscription with the following restrictions: it was to have no more than sixty-six letters, which would be charged at 3½d a letter; it should be in the nature of a text or prayer, and the Commission were to 'have absolute power of rejection or acceptance' over the families' choices since, they asserted, it was 'clearly undesirable to allow free scope for the effusions of the mortuary mason, the sentimental versifier, or the crank'.

Criticism of this last point came from an unusual quarter: *The Times*, inundated with letters of protest from the bereaved, questioned whether it was in fact 'clearly undesirable' to allow families the freedom to say whatever they wanted to in their inscription. It reasoned that:

> The heart of the bereaved may be an epitaph which may seem absurd
> to people in another class of life; nor, by the way, is it at all certain that
> later generations will confirm the judgement of contemporary culture.

The Commission backed down. There is evidence that it did censor inscriptions but it also allowed through some that were both sentimental and surprisingly critical. And *The Times* was right, the hearts of the bereaved are in these epitaphs, and present-day culture does judge differently from the past, infinitely preferring 'A mother's love lies here' to Horace's 'Dulce et decorum est pro patria mori' (It is sweet and fitting to die for one's country).

Epitaphs of the Great War: the Somme is an edited collection of a tiny fraction of these inscriptions. They belong to one hundred soldiers who were killed in action or died of wounds between 1 July and 18 November 1916 during the Somme campaign in which approximately 96,000 British soldiers lost their lives. Many of the dead have no graves and therefore no inscription. This includes some of the well-known dead of the campaign, the author Hector Hugh Munro known as Saki, and the composer George Butterworth. And of those who do have a grave, less than 40 per cent are thought to have an inscription. For some families the cost would have been too great, or they had moved away without a forwarding address, or they just didn't reply. There are no inscriptions on the graves of the musician and rowing champion Frederick Septimus Kelly, or on that of the poet William Noel Hodgson. And there are no inscriptions on any New Zealand headstones. Their Government decided that the necessity for payment infringed the Commission's principle of equality and so refused to allow them. Interestingly, it was for the very same reason that the Canadian Government decided that it would pay for all their soldiers' inscriptions.

This book has come out of my project, Epitaphs of the Great War @WWInscriptions, which Tweets an inscription every day of the First World War Centenary – 4 August 2014 to 11 November 2018. The War Graves Commission's attempt to limit the length of inscriptions to sixty-six characters is more restrictive than Twitter's limit of 140. A blog post accompanies each Tweet, giving the inscription's context. My aim has been to try to take us back into the hearts and minds of those who endured the war and suffered its bereavements, to hear their voice. They convey no single message.

I first visited a war cemetery on my honeymoon and am very grateful to my husband who has uncomplainingly accompanied me on many inscription-collecting expeditions when that was the only way to do it. This was before John Laffin and Trefor Jones published their invaluable collections: *We Will Remember Them: AIF Epitaphs of World War I* and *On Fame's Eternal Camping Ground: A Study of First World War epitaphs in the British cemeteries of the Western Front*, and long before the Commonwealth War Graves Commission published their digitised records as part of their on-going commitment to the commemoration of the war dead. I now have three sons of military-service age – may I never have to choose an inscription for one of them.

Sarah Wearne

Bampton

April 2016

CAPTAIN HOARE'S
HEADSTONE IN
GOMMECOURT
BRITISH CEMETERY
No. 2, HEBUTERNE

"And the Leaves of the Tree Were for the Healing Of the Nations" Rev. XXII.2

CAPTAIN RICHARD LENNARD HOARE
LONDON REGIMENT, THE RANGERS
DIED ON 1ST JULY 1916 AGED 33
BURIED IN GOMMECOURT BRITISH CEMETERY NO. 2, HEBUTERNE, FRANCE

This extract from the Rangers' War Diary, timed and dated 1.30 am 2 July 1916, gives the bare details of Captain Hoare's fate:

> 'C' Company, the centre left element of the attack, had also been hung up on uncut wire. Led by Captain Richard Hoare, who was killed by shrapnel in front of the German lines, the men desperately sought a passage through the German wire and into the relative safety of the German trenches but a hail of rifle fire and bombs was thinning their ranks by the minute.

The regimental history later estimated the casualties for 1 July as fifty-eight per cent:

> There went into action with the Rangers, 23 officers and 780 other ranks. Answered their names at roll call: 6 officers and 280 other ranks.

Richard Hoare's inscription, confirmed by his mother, Laura Hoare, speaks of the new heaven and the new earth that will be a consequence of Christ's eventual triumph over the forces of evil:

> And he shewed me a pure river of water of life, clear as crystal, proceeding out of the throne of God and of the Lamb. In the midst of the street of it, and on either side of the river, was there the tree of life, which bare twelve manner of fruits, and yielded her fruit every month: and the leaves of the tree were for the healing of the nations. Revelation 22:2

HE DIED FOR ULSTER
WE GAVE OUR BEST

PRIVATE RICHARD FOWLER
ROYAL INNISKILLING FUSILIERS
DIED ON 1ST JULY 1916 AGED 19
BURIED IN CONNAUGHT CEMETERY, THIEPVAL, FRANCE

This is a proud and a political inscription. Nineteen-year-old Richard Fowler served with the 9th Battalion the Royal Inniskilling Fusiliers, raised in Omagh, Co. Tyrone in September 1914 from the Tyrone Volunteers. The Tyrone Volunteers were a branch of the Ulster Volunteer Force formed in 1913 and prepared to offer, if necessary, armed resistance to the British Government should it attempt to force through Home Rule for Ireland. Deeply loyal to the British Crown, the Ulster Volunteers raised three battalions for the three Irish regiments drawn from the Six Counties of Ulster: the Royal Inniskilling Fusiliers, the Royal Irish Rifles and the Royal Irish Fusiliers. The combination of Richard Fowler's inscription, his regiment and his home town, Omagh, indicate that he, or at least his parents, were Ulster Unionists if not actually members of the Ulster Volunteers.

The 9th Battalion formed part of the 36th Ulster Division, which performed with great dash, success – and huge casualties – on 1 July 1916. The Battalion War Diary gives the details of the day recalling that:

> Every Officer and Man was eager for the fray & determined to do their utmost that day. All ranks realised that the great test had arrived & that the Honour of Ulster & the reputation of their Regiment was at stake.

The honour of Ulster was upheld on 1 July but the 9th Battalion lost 475 officers and soldiers killed, wounded and missing.

HE SLEEPETH WITH THE BRAVE

LANCE CORPORAL ALAN HILL
BORDER REGIMENT
DIED ON 1ST JULY 1916 AGED 20
BURIED IN BLIGHTY VALLEY CEMETERY, AUTHUILLE WOOD, FRANCE

Alan Hill served with the 11th Battalion the Border Regiment, raised by Lord Lonsdale and known as the Lonsdale Battalion. At 7.30 am on the morning of 1 July the Lonsdales were to leave their trenches in Authuille Wood and follow the Highland Light Infantry Battalion, which had gone over at 7 am, towards the Leipzig Salient. It was estimated that by now the Salient would be in British hands. A witness has them shaking hands with each other and whistling and cheering as they left the trenches. Unfortunately the Leipzig Salient was not in British hands and the Lonsdales were met by deadly fire from the German machine guns. Corporal Hill's inscription references *How Sleep the Brave*, a poem by William Collins, 1721-1759.

> How sleep the brave, who sink to rest
> By all their country's wishes blest!
> When Spring with dewy fingers cold,
> Returns to deck their hallow'd mould,
> She there shall dress a sweeter sod
> Than Fancy's feet have ever trod.
>
> By fairy hands their knell is rung;
> By forms unseen their dirge is sung;
> There Honour comes, a pilgrim grey,
> To bless the turf that wraps their clay;
> And Freedom shall awhile repair
> To dwell, a weeping hermit, there!

Fell in a Righteous Cause
An Englishman and a Jew

PRIVATE ALBERT LAPPIN
ROYAL FUSILIERS
DIED ON 1ST JULY 1916 AGED 19
BURIED IN DANZIG ALLEY BRITISH CEMETERY, MAMETZ, FRANCE

There were many Jews in Britain, especially in London, who had no desire to fight in an army that was allied to Russia. Their families had been the victims of Russian anti-Jewish pogroms and to them Russia was the enemy. The consequent low recruitment figures in Jewish areas fanned the endemic anti-semitism present in some sectors of British society. This was fueled by the suspicion that Jews, who spoke Yiddish, an Eastern European dialect of German, and who had German sounding surnames, were all potential spies.

There were however many Jews who felt grateful to Britain for giving them shelter, and others who had been in Britain since the seventeenth century and felt totally assimilated. It is calculated that by the end of the war, there had been in the region of 41,000 Jewish soldiers in the British Army out of a population of only 280,000.

Albert Lappin lived in Stamford Hill, which is now home to the largest Hasidic community in Europe. By the beginning of the twentieth century prosperous Jews were beginning to move there from the East End of London and Albert's father lived in a substantial three-story house in Osbaldeston Road. I know nothing of their family history, whether they were refugees from Russia or had been in Britain a long time, but in the inscription Albert's father chose for his son he allies himself with Britain's cause, identifies his son as an Englishman but doesn't deny his Jewish faith – a simple but eloquent inscription.

THE WORLD WAS SWEETER FOR HIS LIFE AND LIFE LIVES – POORER BY A FRIEND. A.V.R.

LIEUTENANT ALFRED VICTOR RATCLIFFE
WEST YORKSHIRE REGIMENT
DIED ON 1ST JULY 1916 AGED 29
BURIED IN FRICOURT NEW MILITARY CEMETERY, FRANCE

Alfred Ratcliffe wrote his own epitaph – not for himself but for a friend who died in 1912. The poem, *A Broken Friendship, In Memorian G.C.H.* was written in Harrogate in August 1912 and first published in 1913 in a collection of Ratcliffe's poetry called *A Broken Friendship and Other Verse.* Ratcliffe's mother chose the lines for her son's inscription, although oddly the family later placed a private stone in front of his War Graves headstone, which obscures the original inscription. This plaque reads, 'A very dearly loved son and brother'. The original inscription comes in the last verse of the poem:

> And through the darksome ways of strife
> This thought shall lustre till the end,
> The world was sweeter for his life,
> And life lives – poorer by a friend.

The way the words are laid out on the headstone has led some people to think that they were written 'by a friend' but no, it's that Ratcliffe's life is poorer by the loss of a friend. Ratcliffe, educated at Dulwich College and Sidney Sussex College, Cambridge, was killed on 1 July 1916. His senior officer having been killed earlier in the day, Ratcliffe was commanding the company at the time of his death. A fellow officer told his mother that 'from where we found his body he must have led it pluckily and well'.

I AM THE RESURRECTION
AND THE LIFE

SECOND LIEUTENANT CYRIL HARRY SHEPARD
DEVONSHIRE REGIMENT
1ST JULY 1916 AGED 39
DEVONSHIRE CEMETERY, MAMETZ, FRANCE

> Jesus said unto her, I am the resurrection, and the life: he that believeth
> in me, though he were dead, yet shall he live: And whosoever liveth and
> believeth in me shall never die.
> St John 11: 25-6

Cyril Shepard's inscription, a quote from St John's Gospel, is taken from the opening
words of the Church of England's Order For the Burial of the Dead. Time and again
inscriptions reveal the comfort relations derived from their belief in the Resurrection and
the Christian promise of eternal life.

Cyril Harry Shepard was Ernest Shepard's older brother. Ernest, the illustrator
of *Winnie the Pooh* and *The Wind in the Willows*, served with the Royal Artillery,
Cyril with the 9th Battalion the Devonshire Regiment. In June 1916 both men were
on the Somme, Ernest's guns pounding the German trenches, Cyril and his men
waiting to attack on 1 July. Come the 1st, Cyril and 160 men from the 8th and 9th
Devonshires were killed almost immediately. Many of them caught by a machine
gun positioned exactly where their Company Commander, Captain Martin,
had predicted it would be from the plasticine model he'd made of the terrain.
Later that same day the survivors buried their dead in the same forward trench from
which they had launched their attack, marking the grave with the famous words:

> The Devonshires held this trench
> The Devonshires hold it still

Some days after the battle Ernest found his brother's grave, remarking in his diary that he
was grateful to feel so near to Cyril. He returned several times, telling his wife, Florence,
that 'it's such a strange feeling, I feel as if the place were a kind of home, and I feel
we're kind of greeting each other. I always dream of after the war when you and I can go
there together and I expect Rosemary [Cyril's wife] & Ethel [their sister] will come too.'

Devonshire Cemetery, Mametz: Memorial to members of the Devonshire Regiment killed on 1 July 1916

"THE DEVONSHIRES HELD THIS TRENCH
THE DEVONSHIRES HOLD IT STILL"

1ST JULY 1916
THE 8TH AND 9TH DEVONS
SUFFERED VERY HEAVY CASUALTIES
AS THEY LEFT THEIR FORWARD
TRENCH TO ATTACK

LATER THAT DAY
THE SURVIVORS BURIED THEIR FALLEN
COMRADES IN THAT SAME TRENCH
AND ERECTED A WOODEN MEMORIAL
WITH THE WORDS WHICH ARE
CARVED IN THE CROSS ABOVE

SEMPER FIDELIS

M.A., B.C.L
OF BALLIOL COLLEGE OXFORD
THE DEARLY LOVED SON
OF GUSTAF AND ANNIE ROOS

CAPTAIN GUSTAF OSCAR ROOS
YORK AND LANCASTER REGIMENT
1ST JULY 1916 AGED 47
DOUCHY-LES-AYETTES BRITISH CEMETERY, FRANCE

Gustaf Roos was a well-developed man with auburn hair about 5 foot 9 or 10 inches in height. How do we know? Because this is the description of the body exhumed at Fremicourt Communal Cemetery on 26 June 1924 from underneath a German cross bearing Roos's name.

On 1 July Roos's orders had been to lead 'A' Company 'in file across No Man's Land immediately following assaulting waves. To consolidate and hold German Trench K30a4085 to K23a7510 and to construct and hold strong points A and B along that line'. But this wasn't how it worked, and as the battalion war diary recorded: 'No report of any sort was received back from A or B Companies once they had left Nairne. From reports by wounded men who had got back from No Man's Land, very great casualties were sustained by A and B Companies, while crossing towards the German wire, on the left flank of the attack'.

Later reports suggested that Captain Roos had entered the German trench at the head of his men but had then been wounded, captured by the Germans and died of his wounds in a German hospital three days later. The exhumation report gives an indication of his wounds: 'Both legs broken, body badly smashed'.

Gustaf Roos, a Queen's Scholar at Westminster, took a 1st Class degree in Jurisprudence from Balliol College, Oxford together with a B.C.L., a Bachelor of Civil Law. He worked as a solicitor in London, often acting as 'Poor Man's Solicitor' at Toynbee Hall. He volunteered to fight in the South African War where he was badly wounded. So badly wounded that he found it difficult to persuade anyone to take him seriously when he volunteered to fight in 1914. Eventually, in October 1915, he got a commission in the York and Lancaster Regiment, which is how at the age of 47 he found himself leading 'A' Company across No Man's Land at 7.10 am on the morning of 1 July 1916.

STILL SERVING HIS KING

LANCE CORPORAL CHARLES EDWARD SOPER
LONDON REGIMENT, ROYAL FUSILIERS
DIED ON 1ST JULY 1916 AGED 19
BURIED IN GOMMECOURT BRITISH CEMETERY NO 2, FRANCE

Charles Soper may have given his life for King and Country but the King he was 'still serving' after his death was no longer King George V but it was God, the association made in many popular hymns like George Herbert's 'Teach me my God and King, in all things Thee to see' and his, 'Let all the world in every corner sing, my God and King!' Charles Soper was the son of Thomas Henry Soper of the photographers *Soper and Stedman*. Following their father's death in 1903, his two children, Charles and Cecilia, were sent to the London Orphan Asylum in Watford where children were educated by a charity whose aim was to 'maintain, clothe, and educate respectable fatherless children of either sex, who are without means adequate to their support'. The name makes it sound a terrible place but from the buildings and facilities — chapel, playing fields, infirmary, boarding houses, classrooms — it looks like many a purpose-built, nineteenth-century, neo-Gothic public school. Following a name change in 1939 and a move to Cobham, Surrey after the Second World War, the School is now known as Reeds, an independent day and boarding school.

NOT MY WILL O LORD
BUT THINE BE DONE

PRIVATE THOMAS STAPLETON
LANCASHIRE FUSILIERS
1ST JULY 1916 AGED 38
BURIED IN BLIGHTY VALLEY, AUTHUILLE, FRANCE

The Lord's Prayer appears in both the Gospel of St Matthew 6: 9-13, and in St Luke 11:2-4, but the words most people are and would have been familiar with come from the Book of Common Prayer:

> Our Father, which art in heaven, Hallowed be thy Name, Thy kingdom come, Thy will be done, in earth as it is in heaven. Give us this day our daily bread; And forgive us our trespasses, As we forgive them that trespass against us; And lead us not into temptation, But deliver us from evil. For Thine is the kingdom, the power and the glory, For ever and ever. Amen.

The fourth line, 'Thy will be done', is among the most popular of all personal inscriptions, indicating the bleak acceptance of God's will. However, Private Stapleton's family made it clear that whilst his death may have been God's will, it was not theirs. And this too is a much-used inscription.

The words echo those spoken by Jesus in the hours before his arrest in the Garden of Gethsemene: 'Father, if thou be willing, remove this cup from me: nevertheless not my will, but Thine, be done', St Luke 22:42; 'O my Father, if this cup may not pass away from me, except I drink it, thy will be done, St Matthew 26:42.

I FELL: BUT YIELDED NOT MY ENGLISH SOUL THAT LIVES OUT HERE BENEATH THE BATTLE'S ROLL

SERJEANT JOHN WILLIAM STREETS
YORK AND LANCASTER REGIMENT
1ST JULY 1916 AGED 31
EUSTON ROAD CEMETERY, COLINCAMPS, FRANCE

Serjeant Streets' inscription is a slightly modified quotation from the last lines of one of his own poems, *An English Soldier*, included in a collected edition of his poetry, *The Undying Splendour*:

> He died for love of race; because the blood
> Of northern freemen swelled in his veins; ...
>
> ...
>
> The call of English freemen fled his fears
> And led him (their true son) into the strife.
> There in the van he fought thro' many a dawn,
> Stood by the forlorn hope, knew victory;
> Proud, scorning Death, fought with a purpose drawn
> Sword-edged, defiant, grand, for Liberty.
> He fell; but yielded not his English soul –
> That lives out there beneath the battle's roll.

Streets was killed in the Sheffield Pals' attack on the heavily fortified village of Serre. He was a good soldier, as a senior officer, Major Alfred Plackett, confirmed in a letter to Streets' publisher just before the publication of *Undying Splendour* in May 1917:

> I understand you are publishing a book of the verses of Sergt. J.W. Streets. If his verses are as good as his reputation as a soldier you may rest assured that the book will be a great success. ... He was conspicuous amongst a battalion of brave men who formed the left wing battalion of the great Allied advance on the 1st July. He fell along with the remainder of his comrades, and he died as he had lived ... a MAN. Need I say more? It was a privilege to command such men.

HEART AND SOUL OF A BOY
SIMPLE AND CHEERY
NEVER TO GROW OLD
NEVER GROW WEARY

SECOND LIEUTENANT WALTER HENRY ALEXANDER DAMIANO
ROYAL DUBLIN FUSILIERS
DIED ON 2ND JULY 1916 AGED 19
BURIED IN BEAUVAL COMMUNAL CEMETERY, FRANCE

Walter Damiano's parents capture their nineteen-year-old son's youthful optimism in the first two lines of his inscription, and then express the essence of Laurence Binyon's poem, *For the Fallen*:

> They shall grow not old, as we that are left grow old:
> Age shall not weary them, nor the years condemn.

Damiano, who served with the 2nd Battalion, died of wounds received on the first day of the Battle of the Somme. The Battalion:

> began to advance at 9 am, immediately encountering heavy enfilade fire from Beaumont-Hamel. At 9.05 am two runners arrived and informed Major Walsh, the commanding officer, that the attack was to be postponed. He managed to stop part of C and D companies advancing. However for the rest of the battalion, already in No-Man's-Land, the recall order came too late. At 12 noon, when the order was finally received from Corps HQ to attack and consolidate the position, Walsh reported that this was impossible. Of the twenty-three officers and 480 men who had assembled that morning, fourteen officers and 311 men were now casualties. *The Irish at the Somme* Tim Bowman, *History Ireland* No. 4 Vol. 4 Winter 1996

IT IS A FAR, FAR BETTER THING THAT I DO THAN I HAVE EVER DONE

PRIVATE DAVID BEST
NORTHUMBERLAND FUSILIERS (TYNESIDE SCOTTISH)
DIED ON 3ʳᵈ JULY 1916 AGED 17
BURIED IN ALBERT COMMUNAL CEMETERY EXTENSION, FRANCE

David Best was a seventeen-year-old boy serving with the Tyneside Scottish when he died of wounds on the third day of the Somme campaign. His mother confirmed his inscription. The words come from the last lines of Charles Dickens' *A Tale of Two Cities*, which is set in revolutionary France during the 1790s. They are spoken by the hero, Sydney Carton, who sacrifices his life for the love of a married woman whose husband has been sentenced to death. Carton has the husband rescued and substitutes himself. On his way to the guillotine he tells a companion in the tumbril of his hopes for the future:

> I see a beautiful city and a brilliant people rising from this abyss, and, in their struggles to be truly free, in their triumphs and defeats, through long years to come, I see the evil of this time and of the previous time of which this is the natural birth, gradually making expiation for itself and wearing out. I see the lives for which I lay down my life, peaceful, useful, prosperous and happy, in that England which I shall see no more. ... It is a far, far better thing that I do, than I have ever done; it is a far, far better rest that I go to than I have ever known.

No no no oh God
Not for naught

SECOND LIEUTENANT HAROLD HARDING LINZELL MC
BORDER REGIMENT
DIED ON 3RD JULY 1916 AGED 21
BURIED IN DANZIG ALLEY BRITISH CEMETERY, MAMETZ, FRANCE

Confirmed by Linzell's mother, this inscription sounds like a cry of disbelief, horror and despair, as though Mrs Linzell is railing against God for allowing her son to be killed and pleading with Him that his death shouldn't be in vain. But it's possible that this is not what she meant. There's a hymn by the Scottish hymn writer Horatius Bonar of which these are the first two verses:

> Go, labour on! spend and be spent,
> Thy joy to do the Father's will;
> It is the way the Master went;
> Should not the servant tread it still?

> Go labour on 'tis not for naught
> Thine earthly loss is heavenly gain;
> Men heed thee, love thee, praise thee not;
> The Master praises: what are men?

It is your joy to do God's bidding, why should you not tread the difficult way God's son trod since suffering and sorrow are the way to eternal life.

Linzell kept a diary, which survived his death because of the note inside the front cover:

> In the event of the owner losing this diary or of being "whizz banged, crumped, bombed, bayonetted or sniped" with fatal results to the said person, please forward (risking 'Base Censor') to Mrs F.L. Linzell, Corner House, The Grove, Finchley, London.

Mrs F.L. Linzell was his mother; twenty-one-year old Harold Linzell's wife was called Eva.

'TWERE DISHONOUR TO YIELD OR THE BATTLE TO SHUN

SERJEANT JAMES HENRY WELLS
THE QUEEN'S ROYAL WEST SURREY REGIMENT
DIED ON 3RD JULY 1916 AGED 26
BURIED IN BLIGHTY VALLEY CEMETERY, AUTHUILLE WOOD, FRANCE

Serjeant Wells' inscription comes from the penultimate verse of Thomas B. Pollock's hymn *We Are Soldiers of Christ*, soldiers in the battle against 'satan, the flesh and the world'.

> Now let each cheer his comrade, let hearts beat as one
> While we follow where Christ leads the way;
> 'Twere dishonour to yield, or the battle to shun,
> We will fight, we will watch, we will pray.

Abbot served with the 6th Battalion, which moved into the trenches north-west of Albert on 1 July, in preparation for an attack on the 3rd. Launched at 3.12 am, the attack was in trouble by 4.35 am and ultimately failed. At the end of the day the battalion war diarist attempted to list the reasons for this failure:

- The enemy M.G. whose fire completely swept the ground.
- The enemy wire was insufficiently cut.
- The short time to arrange the attack & not knowing the ground or being able to see the enemy trenches from our parapet, consequent loss of direction.
- The enemy trenches were thick with Germans, so the bombardment cannot have been very successful.

Buried after the battle, Serjeant Wells' grave was lost in the subsequent fighting. But in 1923 a headstone was erected in Blighty Valley Cemetery bearing his name, the inscription his wife chose, and the words 'Believed to be buried in this cemetery'. This is known as a "Special Memorial Type B". These headstones look the same as the usual ones but do not sit over an actual grave. The superscription across the top commemorates men who are buried in the cemetery but whose exact location is unknown or those buried in a grave in another cemetery which is now lost or is unmaintainable.

DEAR HAPPY BOY

SECOND LIEUTENANT JAMES DOUGLAS HODDING
ROYAL FUSILIERS
DIED ON 10TH JULY 1916 AGED 17
BURIED IN HEILLY STATION CEMETERY, MERICOURT-L'ABBE, FRANCE

This 'dear happy boy', a second lieutenant in the 10th Battalion Royal Fusiliers, was born in March 1899, gazetted on 28 May 1915 and therefore was only 17 when he died of wounds at the Casualty Clearing Station in Heilly on 10 July 1916. He was too young to be on active service and too young to be at the front.

Hodding came from a military family, his father, Major James Sweet Hodding, had spent twenty years in the Indian Army, mostly on the North West Frontier. Now living in British Colombia, both father and son joined up on the outbreak of war – as did the youngest brother, Aubrey Vyvian Hodding who served as a trumpeter. However, Aubrey was sent home when it was discovered how young he was – one year younger than his brother James. James Hodding's mother chose his inscription, perhaps influenced by the last words of the poem *Somewhere in France*, written by his friend Ralph Younghusband and dedicated "In loving and affectionate remembrance of my dear friend Lieutenant James Douglas Hodding, who gave his life for his country at the early age of seventeen, at La Boiselle, France, July 10, 1916".

> Somewhere in France, dear comrade, you are lying,
> Beneath a wooden cross, which seems to rise
> Out of an anguished soil, whose fevered crying
> Calls out on God, in pain of sacrifice.
>
> Somewhere in France! My soul goes forth to greet you.
> You are not dead! but only sleep, I know.
> And on the other side, I hope to meet you,
> Dear gallant boy, I loved and cherished so.

OF MANILA
PHILLIPINE ISLANDS
SON OF F.G. DAVIDSON
OF SUEZ, EGYPT

LIEUTENANT GERALD LOUIS DAVIDSON, MC
DORSETSHIRE REGIMENT
DIED ON 11TH JULY 1916 AGED 30
BURIED IN HEILLY STATION CEMETERY, MERICOURT-L'ABBE, FRANCE

London Gazette 25 August 1916

Citation for award of Military Cross to Lieutenant GL Davidson for conspicuous gallantry in action:

He led an attack across the open in daylight to take a strongly fortified 'stop'. His attack was successful and enabled the whole trench to be seized and consolidated. He was twice wounded.

The above action took place on 9 July 1916 during an attack on the German trenches between Mametz Wood and Contalmaison. The British held the trenches but Lieutenant Davidson's wounds were serious and he died two days later at the Casualty Clearing Station in Heilly. Gerald's sister, Helen, signed the form confirming his inscription. It's not clear whether their parents were alive or were still living in Egypt where their father, F.G. Davison, had been an agent for P & O.

Gerald worked in Manila for Messrs Smith, Bell & Co, shipping agents, his eldest brother, Robert, worked in Singapore for Messrs Boustead & Co. Robert served with the Devonshire Regiment and was killed in action on the first day of the battle of the Somme, just ten days before Gerald succumbed to his wounds. Sister Helen chose Robert's inscription too:

Late of the Malay States
Elder son
Of Gerald Davidson
Suez, Egypt.

NB The spelling of Phillipine in the inscription is as it was signed for on the form.

I HAVE FELT
WITH MY NATIVE LAND
I AM ONE WITH MY KIND

SERJEANT FRANCIS ALBERT HAWES
ROYAL GARRISON ARTILLERY
DIED ON 11TH JULY 1916 AGED 25
BURIED IN HERSIN COMMUNAL CEMETERY EXTENSION, FRANCE

Serjeant Francis Albert Hawes was the son of a professional soldier, Staff Serjeant Francis Anthony Hawes, who chose this inscription. It comes from the penultimate line of Alfred, Lord Tennyson's poem, Maud.

For all the hilarity caused by its most famous line: 'Come into the garden Maud', this is a dark, cynical and controversial poem. This is unlikely to be the reason Francis Anthony Hawes chose it. More likely he appreciated the last two stanzas, which tell of a country (Britain) that has lost for a little its lust for gold, and its love for 'a peace that was full of wrongs and shame', and is prepared to embrace war in order that 'God's just wrath shall be wreak'd on a giant liar'. Tennyson's 'giant liar' was Russia and his war the Crimean War but many will have thought the words equally applicable to the Great War. Now, 'The blood-red blossom of war with a heart of fire' has begun to burn:

> Let it flame or fade, and the war roll down like a wind,
> We have proved we have hearts in a cause, we are noble still
> And myself have awaked, as it seems, to the better mind
> It is better to fight for the good, than to rail at the ill;
> I have felt with my native land, I am one with my kind,
> I embrace the purpose of God, and the doom assign'd.

Tell England
That we who died
Serving her
Rest here content

CAPTAIN MARCUS HERBERT GOODALL
YORK AND LANCASTER REGIMENT
DIED ON 14TH JULY 1916 AGED 21
BURIED IN PUCHEVILLERS BRITISH CEMETERY, FRANCE

This is an epitaph with a long history and a deep emotional resonance. It derives from the epitaph said to have been written by Simonides to mark the graves of the Spartans who fell with Leonidas at Thermopylae in 480 BC: 'O passer by, tell the Lacedaemonians that we lie here obeying their orders.' The words were adapted and used on a memorial to the men of the Imperial Light Horse killed at Waggon Hill, South Africa on 6 January 1900.

> Tell England, ye who pass this monument
> We, who died serving her, rest here content.

Marcus Goodall makes an appearance as Lieutenant Allgood in Siegfried Sassoon's *Memoirs of an Infantry Officer*. Like everyone, Goodall is disguised by a pseudonym but Sassoon is not thought to have disguised people's characters:

> Allgood was quiet, thoughtful, and fond of watching birds. We had been to the same public school, though there were nearly ten years between us. He told me that he wanted to be a historian, and I listened respectfully while he talked about the Romans in Early Britain, which was his favourite subject. ... Allgood never grumbled about the war, for he was a gentle soul, willing to take his share in it, though obviously unsuited to homicide. But there was an air of veiled melancholy on his face, as if he were inwardly warned that he would never see his home in Wiltshire again. A couple of months afterwards I saw his name on one of the long lists of killed, and it seemed to me that he had expected it.

'Though obviously not suited to homicide', in those six words Sassoon encapsulates the predicament of so many young men who not only had to be willing to die for their country but to kill for it too.

BORN IN EDINBURGH HE FOUGHT FOR SCOTLAND AND FOR SOUTH AFRICA

PRIVATE ALEXANDER TOD
SOUTH AFRICAN INFANTRY
DIED BETWEEN 15TH AND 20TH JULY 1916 AGED 36
BURIED IN LONDON CEMETERY AND EXTENSION, LONGUEVILLE, FRANCE

Private Alexander Tod served with the 3rd South African Regiment, which attacked with the South African Brigade at Delville Wood, 'a corner of death', on 15 July 1916. When the Brigade withdrew on the 20th, after a titanic struggle, two thirds of the Brigade had become casualties. The *History of South Africa in the Great War* summed up the episode:

> The six days and five nights during which the South African Brigade held the most difficult post on the British front – a corner of death on which the enemy fire was concentrated at all hours from three sides, and into which fresh German troops, vastly superior in numbers to the defence, made periodic incursions only to be broken and driven back – constitutes an epoch of terror and glory scarcely equalled in the campaign.

Alexander Tod went into battle on the 15th and didn't answer at roll call on the 20th, no one could tell exactly when he was killed, which is why his date of death is given as 'Between 15/07/1916 and 20/07/1916' in the War Graves Commission's records. For eighteen years his fate was 'missing, believed killed in action'. Until 1934 when three bodies in a single grave were discovered at map reference 57c.5.18.b.65.20. Tod still had his identity disc and so could be buried in a named grave; the other two men were reburied as unidentified British soldiers – UBSs. By 1934 both Tod's parents were dead and it was his sister in Edinburgh who chose his inscription. She makes no bones about where her brother's loyalties had lain – 'He fought for Scotland and for South Africa'.

FAR DISTANT, FAR DISTANT
LIES SCOTIA THE BRAVE
HERE LIES A TRUE HIGHLANDER

DRIVER HECTOR MACMILLAN
ROYAL FIELD ARTILLERY
DIED ON 16TH JULY 1916 AGED 26
BURIED IN DIVE COPSE BRITISH CEMETERY, SAILLY-LE-SEC, FRANCE

Hector Macmillan's inscription comes from the first line of a traditional Scottish song, *Jamie Foyers*.

> Far distant, far distant, lies Scotia the brave,
> No tombstone memorial shall hallow his grave,
> His bones they are scattered on the rude soil of Spain,
> For young Jamie Foyers in the battle was slain.

Jamie Foyers was a real soldier from Campsie in Stirlingshire who died in 1812 fighting in the Duke of Wellington's army at the siege of Burgos during the Peninsula Wars.

Hector Macmillan was born in 1890 in Campbeltown, Kintyre, making him by definition a highlander. He enlisted in August 1914 on the outbreak of war and served as a driver with the 9th Divisional Ammunition Column Royal Field Artillery. He was killed in action between Maricourt and Carnoy during the Battle of Delville Wood.

FRAMED IN THE PRODIGALITY OF NATURE YOUNG, VALIANT, WISE

LIEUTENANT ERNEST EMANUEL POLACK
GLOUCESTERSHIRE REGIMENT
DIED ON 17TH JULY 1916 AGED 23
BURIED IN LONSDALE CEMETERY, AUTHUILLE, FRANCE

With these words, Shakespeare's Richard III describes the young prince Edward of Westminster, killed fighting for the Lancastrians at the Battle of Tewkesbury in 1471:

> A sweeter and lovelier gentleman,
> Framed in the prodigality of nature,
> Young, valiant, wise and, no doubt, right royal,
> The spacious world cannot again afford;

Ernest's father, Joseph Polack, chose this inscription. Joseph was a schoolmaster, a Jewish minister, and the master of the Jewish boarding house at Clifton College, Bristol. Joseph's parents, German Jews, had been born in Hamburg and come to England in 1853. Two letters from Ernest Polack survive, both published in Laurence Weaver's *War Letters of Fallen Englishmen*, and in both of them Ernest quotes Shakespeare: *Much Ado About Nothing* to the father of a friend killed in action, and *Anthony and Cleopatra*, *Julius Caesar*, and *Hamlet* in his last letter to his parents, the letter in which he leaves his Shakespeare books to his twin brother, Albert. Ernest had just completed two years at St John's College, Cambridge when the war broke out. He joined up immediately and was commissioned into the Gloucestershire Regiment, going to Flanders in April the following year. His last letter was composed in the knowledge that the Somme offensive was about to start and that he might not get through it – at least not whole. He reassures his parents that death has no terrors for him, although the prospect of pain appals him, which is why he tells them that he will be taking morphia with him into battle before concluding, 'Our cause is a good one and I believe I am doing right in fighting. ... Goodbye! "If we meet again, why then we'll smile. If not – why then this parting was well made".' This last comes from *Julius Caesar* and is Cassius's farewell to Brutus before the Battle of Philippi. An older brother, Benjamin Polack, died in Mesopotamia on 9 April 1916, he has no grave and is commemorated on the Basra Memorial in Iraq.

'IF WE ARE MARKED TO DIE
WE ARE ENOUGH
TO DO OUR COUNTRY LOSS'
HENRY V

PRIVATE JOHN HENRY RAYNER
MIDDLESEX REGIMENT
DIED ON 17TH JULY 1916 AGED 23
BURIED IN DIVE COPSE BRITISH CEMETERY, SAILLY-LE-SEC, FRANCE

John Rayner's parents chose a quotation from Shakespeare's *Henry V* for their son's inscription. On the eve of the Battle of Agincourt, King Henry, overhearing the Earl of Westmoreland lament the fact that the English Army is so small, tells him that he would not wish for one man more: if we are all about to die then there are quite enough of us to 'do our country loss', but if we are going to live then there will be fewer people for us to have to share the honour with. This is the beginning of Henry's famous St Crispin's Day speech in which he assures his listeners that 'From this day to the ending of the world, but we in it shall be remembered: We few, we happy few, we band of brothers'. John Henry Rayner, a warehouseman from Islington, was his parents' only child. From the location of his grave, Dives Copse was adjacent to a collection of Field Ambulance stations, he must have died of wounds before getting very far down the casualty evacuation chain.

LALA-GAHLE, UMTA-GWETU
PRO ARIS ET FOCIS

SECOND LIEUTENANT AYLMER TEMPLAR WALES
SOUTH AFRICAN INFANTRY
DIED ON 17TH JULY 1916 AGED 22
BURIED IN DIVE COPSE BRITISH CEMETERY, SAILLY-LE-SEC, FRANCE

The first line of this inscription is in Zulu. The word 'gahle' has been spelt phonetically and would now be spelt 'kahle'. 'Lala-gahle' therefore means 'good-night'. 'Umta-gwetu' means sleep well.

The second line of the inscription is the Latin motto of Maritzburg College, the school Aylmer Wales attended in Pietermartzburg, Natal. It comes from Cicero's *De Natura Deorum* and translates as, for our altars and fires. This of course means much more than just altars and fires, it is what the Romans held most sacred, most worth defending, the equivalent of hearth and home, King and country.

Lieutenant-Colonel ATG Wales, Aymer Wales' father, made a point of recording in the cemetery register that his son, a non-commissioned officer, had been 'commissioned on the field' just before his death. Officer casualties had been so great during this period that immediate commissioning from the ranks was necessary to maintain the chain of command. Second Lieutenant Wales died of wounds received at Delville Wood on the third day of the battle.

DID HE DIE IN VAIN?

PRIVATE JOHN PAUL
SOUTH AFRICAN INFANTRY
DIED ON 18TH JULY 1916 AGED 36
BURIED IN LONDON CEMETERY AND EXTENSION, LONGUEVILLE, FRANCE

Private Paul's wife asks an unusually direct question: 'Did he die in vain?' Whilst not actually asserting that he did, the mere fact that she has asked the question is significant. Paul, serving with the South African Infantry, was killed at Delville Wood when the South African Brigade suffered huge casualties – two thirds killed, wounded and missing. Paul was initially among the missing. It was not until February 1935 that his body was located at map reference 57c.S.18.s.45.90, exhumed and reinterred in London Road Cemetery and Extension, Longueville, where 3,114 of the 3,873 burials are unidentified. Originally among the unidentified, Paul was later identified by his knife and fork, which were marked J. Paul, and by his general service tunic, kilt and boots.

His kilt? John Paul, born in Scotland, had emigrated to South Africa from where he volunteered to serve with 4th Regiment the South African Infantry, the South African Scottish. Raised from the Transvaal Scottish and Cape Town Highlanders, they wore kilts of the Atholl Murray tartan.

Interestingly, it could be the long delay between Private Paul's death and the discovery of his body that explains the suggested negativity of his inscription. The economic depression, unemployment, the deteriorating situation in Europe and the publication of Sassoon's, Graves' and other anti-war memoirs had by now caused some to question the cause for which their menfolk had died. It appears that Mrs Florence Paul might have been among them.

LEGION D'HONNEUR
IN REMEMBRANCE OF MY
BELOVED HUSBAND
AND IN GLORIOUS EXPECTATION

MAJOR WILLIAM LA TOUCHE CONGREVE, VC, DSO, MC
RIFLE BRIGADE
DIED ON 20TH JULY 1916 AGED 25
BURIED IN CORBIE COMMUNAL CEMETERY EXTENSION, FRANCE

Billy Congreve had been the 'beloved husband' of his wife, Pamela, for exactly seven weeks before he was killed by a sniper. Just 25 when he died, he was thought to have a great military future being bold, resourceful, utterly dedicated and a natural leader, qualities which played their part in the Victoria Cross he was awarded for his actions during the two weeks before his death – constantly performing acts of gallantry and 'by his personal example inspiring all those around him with confidence at critical periods during the operations'. The previous October, Congreve had been awarded the Croix de Chevalier, Légion d'Honneur, France's highest decoration. Both Congreve's parents served in the war, his mother as a nurse in the Red Cross, and his father, Lieutenant-General Walter Congreve VC, as commander of XIII Corps during the Battle of the Somme. Serving in the same theatre of war meant that the two men were able to see something of each other before Billy was killed, and Walter Congreve was able to visit his dead son before he was buried:

> [I] was struck by his beauty and strength of face … I never felt so proud
> of him as I did when I said goodbye to him. I myself put in his hand
> a posy of poppies, cornflowers and daisies … and with a kiss I left him.

One of Congreve's fellow officers wrote to Pamela Congreve, 'I don't think there was ever anyone like him; he was absolutely glorious, and even when he was ADC, all the men knew and loved him – which is unusual'. Mrs Congreve used the word glorious in his headstone inscription – 'in glorious expectation'. When her husband died she was expecting a baby. The baby was born on 21 March 1917 and named Mary Gloria.

THE NOBLE ARMY OF MARTYRS PRAISE THEE

SECOND LIEUTENANT ROBERT ASTLEY FRANKLIN EMINSON
KING'S ROYAL RIFLE CORPS
DIED ON 20TH JULY 1916 AGED 24
BURIED IN BECOURT MILITARY CEMETERY, BECORDEL-BECOURT, FRANCE

Robert Eminson's inscription comes from the *Te Deum Laudamus*, a hymn of praise to God that forms a regular part of the Church of England's service of Matins.

> We praise thee, O God: we acknowledge thee to be the Lord.
> All the earth doth worship thee: the father everlasting. ...
> The glorious company of the Apostles: praise thee.
> The goodly fellowship of the Prophets: praise thee.
> The noble army of Martyrs: praise thee.
> The holy Church throughout all the world: doth acknowledge thee; ...

Eminson was a Cambridge educated entomologist conducting research into the tsetse fly in Rhodesia (Zimbabwe) when the war broke out. He returned home to join up in January 1915 and was killed in July the following year trying to bring in a wounded man. Various eyewitness accounts describe the circumstances:

> - There were a good many casualties and on the following morning your son observed a wounded man lying outside the trench, unable to get in by himself. He at once crawled out to him but found there would be some difficulty in getting him through the wire. It was after going out for the third time to reconnoitre a way in through the wire that the enemy machine gun caught him. The Battalion doctor went out to see if he could do anything, but your son was already dead.

> - The wounded man was Sergeant Samuel Yerrell of the Northants. With both arms shattered by a bomb, he was helped back to the lines. Too exhausted to negotiate the barbed wire, he collapsed. Then a Second Lieutenant jumped out of our trench and went to help them ... a German fired at them, the bullet passing through Sam's back and right through the officer's heart. The officer was killed instantly, and poor Sam died an hour later... The brave officer... was Lieutenant Eminson.

FOR ENGLAND

LIEUTENANT RICHARD ROY LEWER
KING'S ROYAL RIFLE CORPS
DIED ON 21ST JULY 1916 AGED 26
BURIED IN HEILLY STATION CEMETERY, MERICOURT-L'ABBE, FRANCE

Richard Lewer, in civilian life a geological surveyor, was wounded on 16 July 1916 in the King's Royal Rifle Corps' attack on High Wood. He lay out in the open for four days before being found. A brother officer and a fellow old boy of Denstone College, who was wounded on the 15th, takes up the story:

> On the 20th he [Lewer] was brought into No. 36 Casualty Clearing Station and put into the bed opposite mine (later we were moved and I was next to him). He was very weak of course, and asked for food but was quite cheery. We then exchanged experiences.
>
> When he was hit his orderly got him into a shell-hole, bandaged him up and put a rough splint on his leg. Then they withdrew and he couldn't be got away. His orderly had to go and left his water-bottle with him. He was in the shell-hole five days (16th to 20th) until we took the wood again. When the Germans came in they didn't take any notice of him but he told them to give him some water, which they did, but no food. After the first day they wouldn't give him anything, and then left him alone, except to call him names so that he then had about two bottles of water (his orderly's and his) left, which he spun out.
>
> His wound didn't trouble him very much, and he had morphia with him which he took periodically. This of course was a great relief and enabled him to sleep a certain amount. The worst thing of all, was, of course, when our guns shelled the wood, which was pretty often, and it is wonderful that he was not hit again. Then on the 20th he was found by our own people, much to everyone's surprise, and got back immediately. This is all he told me; he was asleep when I was moved so I couldn't say good-bye. Later of course, he died of his wounds.
> *The Denstonian* April 1917

Lewer was a geological surveyor who had worked for British Burmah Oil Co. before going to the Caucasian Oil Fields and then to Western Canada. He returned to Britain immediately on the outbreak of war and was commissioned into the King's Royal Rifle Corps.

WELL PLAYED! LAD

RIFLEMAN SAMUEL GUNN
KING'S ROYAL RIFLE CORPS
DIED ON 27TH JULY 1916 AGED 20
BURIED IN DIVE COPSE BRITISH CEMETERY, SAILLY-LE-SEC, FRANCE

'Well played! Lad' is more the sort of thing you say to someone as they come off the pitch having made a century, or scored the winning goal, than put on a headstone inscription: war is hardly a game. Much scorn has been poured on the association of sport with war, derived from the public schools and epitomized in Henry Newbolt's poem *Vitaï Lampada*. Here, at a desperate moment during a desert battle in the Sudanese War of 1885:

> The river of death has brimmed his banks,
> And England's far, and Honour a name,
> But the voice of a schoolboy rallies the ranks:
> "Play up! Play up! and play the game!"

Samuel Gunn did not go to a public school. At the age of 14 he was already working in his father's home-based, hosiery-manufacturing business in Ruddington, Nottinghamshire. His mother confirmed his inscription. It speaks of affectionate approval for a task well performed but does undoubtedly associate war with sport. However, neither Newbolt nor Mrs Gunn meant that war was actually a game, rather that the qualities of a good sportsman could be seen in a good soldier. Samuel's family came from Nottinghamshire where there was a famous sporting family called Gunn. This included William Gunn and his nephews John and George who all played cricket for Nottinghamshire and England in the early years of the twentieth century. However, despite the same surname and Samuel Gunn's sporting inscription, there does not seem to be a family connection. Gunn served with the 1st Battalion The King's Royal Rifle Corps and was killed on 27 July 1916 in defending a determined German counter-attack at Delville Wood.

HE DIED AS HE LIVED
BRAVE AND FEARLESS

LIEUTENANT ALAN SCRIVENER LLOYD MC
ROYAL FIELD ARTILLERY
DIED ON 4TH AUGUST 1916 AGED 27
BURIED IN DARTMOOR CEMETERY, BECORDEL-BECOURT, FRANCE

Lieutenant Lloyd was killed reconnecting the wire from his forward observation post, which had been broken by a German bombardment. Some weeks after his death, Gunner John Manning, who had been with Lloyd when he died, placed a small hand-made, wooden sign on Lloyd's grave on which he had written, 'He died as he lived, brave and fearless, a true British hero'. Lloyd's wife chose the first eight words for her husband's headstone inscription. The wooden sign is now part of the Imperial War Museum Collection, as are many of Lloyd's papers. Lloyd was a Quaker, educated at Leighton Park School and Trinity College, Cambridge. He fell out with his parents over his decision to enlist, but as he wrote in a letter to his father:

> Everybody must put their personal considerations in the background now, & I don't believe you'd be so selfish as to try & stop me doing my part. Possibly you don't realize that this is a life & death struggle with Germany. Everybody who could do something & won't is a beastly unpatriotic kind of person. I'm the last person to be a Jingo & hate flag-wagging and Union Jack hurrahing etc but do feel that I might be useful, with my motor or without it, in case of attack by Germany and so I've offered my services ...

Alan Lloyd was one of four brothers. Two of them originally joined the Friends Ambulance Unit but after their brother's death one joined the navy and the other the army. The third brother was a conscientious objector.

TALL, EAGER
A FACE TO REMEMBER
A SPIRIT
THAT BRIGHTENED OUR HOME

SERGEANT ALLAN FREDERICK BATH
AUSTRALIAN INFANTRY
DIED ON 5TH AUGUST 1916 AGED 20
BURIED IN SERRE ROAD CEMETERY NO. 2, SERRE, FRANCE

This inscription is a near quote from a poem titled *P.L.C.* in *Harrow Songs & Other Verses*, 1886, by Edward E. Bowen, of which these are the opening lines.

> Not surely a week since we saw him,
> Health brimming in feature and limb;
> Let me try to imagine and draw him,
> Ere fancy and feature are dim.
> Tall, eager, a face to remember,
> A flush that could change as the day;
> A spirit that knew not December,
> That brightened the sunshine of May.

Bowen's book sold few copies, but Horace Vachell quoted the poem in his novel *The Hill, a Romance of Friendship*, which was published in 1905 and had phenomenal worldwide sales. This is how the poem became well known. Allan Bath was a market gardener from Burwood, Victoria, Australia. Although the War Graves Commission has his age at death as 25, his father has written 'twenty years' on the circular for the Roll of Honour of Australia. And beside the question asking if there are any other details likely to be of interest to the historians he writes: 'Two letters found in his knapsack from his Captain and Major at Etaples recommending him for Lieutenancy'. Bath was killed at Pozieres on 5 August 1916. His body was not discovered until March 1929 when, as it still had his identity disc and a piece of tobacco pouch engraved with the initials AB, it was possible to bury him under a named headstone. Mr F Bath confirmed his inscription; this was not his father, William Bath, who may well have been dead by then.

An Australian hero

PRIVATE HAROLD ROY BENZLEY
AUSTRALIAN INFANTRY
DIED ON 6TH AUGUST 1916 AGED 20
BURIED IN PUCHEVILLERS BRITISH CEMETERY, FRANCE

This Australian hero, a clerk from Sunbury, Victoria, enlisted on 12 May 1915 and embarked from Melbourne for Egypt on 16 July 1915. Sent to Gallipoli at the end of August, he was on board the *Southland* when it was torpedoed in the Aegean by UB-14 on 2 September 1915. His war record lists a catalogue of hospitalizations:

> Admitted to 6th Australian Field Ambulance, Anzac, 31 October 1915 (influenza); transferred to 1st Australian Casualty Clearing Station, Anzac, 3 November 1915 (enteric); evacuated and disembarked Alexandria, 9 November 1915; admitted to No 15 General Hospital, Alexandria, 9 November 1915; proceeded to England, 16 November 1915; admitted to County of London War Hospital, Epsom, England, 27 November 1915. Proceeded overseas to France, 7 June 1916;

Two months later, Benzley was 'admitted at this station [3rd Casualty Clearing Station] 6th August 1916 suffering from gun shot wounds head, with compound fracture of skull. He died the same day'.

A hero may be defined as someone who is admired for their courage and their brave actions, but never forget R.C. Sherriff's definition in *Journey's End*. The main character, Captain Stanhope, is thought by his men to be a hero, but as he openly confesses to Lieutenant Hibbert, who is terrified of the forthcoming action and trying to get out of it by feigning illness:

> Sometimes I feel I could just lie down on this bed and pretend I was paralysed or something – and couldn't move – and just lie there till I died – or was dragged away. But others are sticking it so we have to too. Don't you think it worth standing in with men like that? – when you know they all feel like you do – in their hearts – and just go on sticking it because they know it's – it's the only thing a decent man can do.

A MOTHER'S LOVE LIES HERE

PRIVATE WILLIAM OGSTON CRAIB
AUSTRALIAN INFANTRY
DIED ON 6TH AUGUST 1916 AGED 28
BURIED IN PUCHEVILLERS BRITISH CEMETERY, FRANCE

Aberdeen Evening Express 16 August 1916
Mrs Craib, 52a Virginia Street, Aberdeen, has today received a letter from the Presbyterian chaplain with the Australian force in France intimating the death of her second son, Lance-Corporal William Ogston Craib, 26th Battalion, A.I.F. He was wounded on August 5 in action, and died on the following day. He left Aberdeen about four years ago for Brisbane, Queensland, and was engaged as a fireman there. Shortly after the outbreak of war he enlisted in the Australian force, and took part in the Dardanelles campaign. Lance-Corporal Craib was 28 years of age. Mrs Craib's other son, Private George Craib, H.L.I., was killed at the battle of Loos on 25th September. He served through the South African War, and rejoined his old regiment in September 1914

Aberdeen Evening Express 4 April 1916
Another death among Aberdeen soldiers at the battle of Loos, on September 25 last has now been announced to the relatives. The soldier was Private George Craib elder son of Mr and Mrs George Craib, 52a Virginia Street, Aberdeen. He had previously been reported wounded and afterwards missing. Private Craib was 42 years of age. He joined the colours in September 1914, after having previously served for eleven years, his unit at the time being the 2nd Battalion Highland Light Infantry in which he went through the Tirah expedition and the South African War. Prior to the outbreak of the present war he was a trawl fisherman. His brother Private Willliam Craib took part with the Australian contingent in the Daradenelles campaign and is now serving elsewhere.

George Craib's body was never found so he has no grave and no inscription. He is commemorated on the Loos Memorial.

OUR LAD
RUDDY OF HAIR
AND STRONG OF LIMB

PRIVATE LEWIS NORMAN SHEPHERD
AUSTRALIAN INFANTRY
DIED ON 8TH AUGUST 1916 AGED 23
BURIED IN PUCHEVILLERS BRITISH CEMETERY, FRANCE

This tender inscription, chosen by Lewis Shepherd's mother, provides a vivid picture of this well built, red haired, twenty-three-year-old butcher from Penguin in Tasmania who died of wounds at a Casualty Clearing Station in Puchevillers. Whilst it is obvious that 'ruddy' means red haired, the word also carries other connotations: youthful, fresh complexioned and in the case of David, Jesse's youngest and best beloved son, 'of a beautiful countenance', 1 Samuel 16:12.

On 2 January 1917, five months after Lewis died, his brother Ernest Victor Shepherd was killed in action at Armentieres. Their mother chose his inscription too:

Beloved
He is not dead
He is just away

IN DREAMS WE SEE YOU
ON THE BATTLE PLAIN
WOUNDED, CALLING IN VAIN

PRIVATE LYELL POCOCK
AUSTRALIAN INFANTRY
DIED ON 15TH AUGUST 1916 AGED 17
BURIED IN BECOURT MILITARY CEMETERY, BECORDEL-BECOURT, FRANCE

This is surely no dream, the vision of your seventeen-year-old son lying wounded on the battlefield, calling in vain for help, is the stuff of nightmares not dreams. Lyell Pocock was wounded on 15 August during the Battle of Pozieres and died the same day. His parents never instituted a search by the Red Cross Wounded and so there is no record of the circumstances of his death but Mr and Mr James Pocock were obviously haunted by their fears. These were represented in the words of the popular song from which they chose his inscription.

When This Cruel War is Over, written in 1862 and dedicated to 'Sorrowing hearts at home', was the most popular song of the American Civil War whether with Unionists or Confederates. Lyell Pocock's inscription is an adaptation of the second and third verses:

> When the summer breeze is sighing, mournfully along,
> Or when autumn leaves are falling, sadly breathes the song.
> Oft in dreams I see thee lying on the battle plain,
> Lonely, wounded, even dying, calling but in vain.
>
> If amid the din of battle, nobly you should fall,
> Far away from those who love you, none to hear you call –
> Who would whisper words of comfort, who would soothe your pain?
> Ah! the many cruel fancies, ever in my brain.

Whilst the announcement of his death in the local Bendigo papers described Lyell as 18, James Pocock was very precise when he filled in the circular for the Roll of Honour of Australia: his son was 'seventeen and six months'. This means that he was sixteen and five months when he enlisted in September 1915, and still sixteen when he embarked from Australia on 25 January 1916.

THE LORD GAVE
THE LORD HATH TAKEN AWAY
BLESSED BE
THE NAME OF THE LORD

CAPTAIN BASIL HALLAM RADFORD
ROYAL FLYING CORPS
DIED ON 20TH AUGUST 1916 AGED 28
BURIED IN COUIN BRITISH CEMETERY, FRANCE

These are Job's words, Job 1:21-2, after God has tested him to the limit by taking away his wealth, his possessions and finally his children. It's a sober inscription for the man the public knew as Basil Hallam, the idol of the English stage, who played the fop Gilbert the Filbert the Knut with a K alongside the sensational American revue star, Elsie Janis, in *The Passing Show 1914* at the Palace Theatre, London. More than fifty years after his death, Cecil Beaton remembered Hallam as having 'an attraction that was devastating to all ages and sexes'.

Hallam left *The Passing Show* after the sinking of the Lusitania on 7 May 1915. Americans in London were outraged and conflicted, could/would/should the US maintain her neutrality? Elsie declared that she was about as neutral as 'cyanide of potassium'. The couple left the show together, Elsie describing their last night as making 'any opening night I have ever had seem colourless by comparison'.

Hallam joined the Royal Flying Corps and served in the Kite Balloon section in the skies over the Somme where, just over a year later, he was killed falling from his balloon. Despite the fact that hundreds must have seen him fall, the facts are disputed. Was the balloon being pulled in when it broke away, did it break loose in a high wind or was it brought down by enemy fire? Were there two men or three on board; was Hallam wearing a parachute, which snagged, or did he not have one? Gerald Gliddon, writing authoritatively for the Western Front Association, states that the balloon broke free in the wind and that Hallam had no parachute. Balloon crew, unlike pilots, were provided with parachutes, one for each man, the pilot and the observer. But there were three men in the balloon that day; there was a friend with them who had gone for the ride. Hallam gave the friend his parachute and jumped rather than fall into enemy hands. Raymond Asquith, the son of British Prime Minister Herbert Asquith, who was among those who watched it happen, described it as 'a frightening death, even to look at'.

HERE LIES A FATHER'S HOPE
A MOTHER'S PRIDE
AND A WIFE'S DEPENDENCE

PRIVATE JOHN PRENTICE
THE CAMERONIANS SCOTTISH RIFLES
DIED ON 23RD AUGUST 1916 AGED 27
BURIED IN BECOURT MILITARY CEMETERY, BECORDEL-BECOURT, FRANCE

In twelve simple words James Prentice describes a world of loss: for himself, his wife and his son's wife, Robina – a father's hope, a mother's pride and a wife's dependence, her financial security.

On the 19 August the 10th Battalion went into the trenches opposite Becourt Wood. Three soldiers from the battalion died whilst they were still there on 23 August, two were buried beside Field Ambulance stations and one is commemorated on the Thiepval Memorial. There is no record of what caused their deaths.

War widows did receive a pension: 20 shillings a week if there were no children. By the time Becourt Military Cemetery was finalised in 1933 Robina Prentice had re-married.

LIFE'S WORK WELL DONE
LIFE'S VICTORY WON
NOW COMES REST

CORPORAL PERCY CHARLES BUFFIN
OXFORDSHIRE AND BUCKINGHAMSHIRE LIGHT INFANTRY
DIED ON 24TH AUGUST 1916 AGED 24
BURIED IN DELVILLE WOOD CEMETERY, LONGUEVAL, FRANCE

This inscription has a strange history. It comes from the first verse of a poem written in America in 1879 by Edward H. Parker for the funeral of a friend. He based it on the words from The Epistle of St Paul to the Hebrews 4:9, 'There remaineth therefore a rest to the people of God'. Translated into Latin by another friend, W.H. Crosby, both the English and Latin versions were published in the New York Observer on 13 May 1880. There was no further publicity until over a year later when, much to Parker's surprise, a slightly amended first verse appeared on the coffin of the assassinated President James Garfield.

> Life's race well run,
> Life's work well done,
> Life's crown well won,
> Now comes rest.

Following a clamour in the newspapers, the author of these lines was eventually traced back to Edward H. Parker. Although Parker's original first verse was slightly different:

> Life's race well run,
> Life's work all done,
> Life's victory won,
> Now cometh rest.

This is the version that was picked up, circulated and became extremely popular all over the world. Like many parents, Percy Charles Buffin's thought it an appropriate inscription for their soldier son. Father, Frederick Buffin, owned a grocery business at 455 Kings Road, Chelsea, Percy, one of five children, was an apprentice printer. Aged 17 in 1909 he joined the London Division, Territorial Force, so that when war came in 1914 he was a trained soldier. He served with the 5th Battalion the Oxfordshire and Buckinghamshire Light Infantry and was killed at Delville Wood on 24 August 1916.

DELVILLE WOOD
CEMETERY, LONGUEVAL

OUR BUGLES SANG TRUCE

PRIVATE JAMES DUFF CAMPBELL
ROYAL SCOTS
DIED ON 28TH AUGUST 1916 AGED 24
BURIED CATERPILLAR VALLEY CEMETERY, LONGUEVAL, FRANCE

Private Campbell's mother chose his inscription. It comes from the first line of *The Soldier's Dream* by Thomas Campbell (1777-1844). The poem became popular during the Crimean War (1853-56), was included in 1875 in Palgrave's best-selling *Golden Treasury* collection and became the subject of a Staffordshire ceramic figurine, which shows a highland soldier sleeping beside his cannon.

> Our bugles sang truce, for the night-cloud had lower'd,
> And the sentinel stars set their watch in the sky;
> And thousands had sunk on the ground overpower'd,
> The weary to sleep, and the wounded to die.

And what was the soldier's dream?

> Methought from the battlefield's dreadful array
> Far, far I had roam'd on a desolate track:
> 'Twas Autumn, and sunshine arose on the way
> To the home of my fathers, that welcomed me back.

Surrounded by the sights and sounds of his home and his loved ones, the soldier vows never to leave it again. But then he wakes up and realises that it was all just a dream.

> But sorrow return'd with the dawning of morn,
> And the voice in my dreaming ear melted away.

James Campbell served with the 13th Battalion the Royal Scots, a New Army battalion. He was killed in action near High Wood where the Regiment's casualties from German shelling were in the region of thirty a day.

AT REST IN PEACE

PRIVATE ROBERT ANDREW LOMAX PURVES
ROYAL SCOTS
DIED ON 29TH AUGUST 1916 AGED 31
BURIED IN DANZIG ALLEY BRITISH CEMETERY, MAMETZ, FRANCE

This inscription isn't a request by Robert Purves's father that his son may rest in peace but a statement that his son IS at rest in peace. Why do I think so? Read this ...

> I have shot myself as I cannot stand the hardship & sufferings of this life any longer, and there is no chance of getting home to see my parents whom may God bless and comfort in their trouble. Mr Clarkson and Mr Collins are two fine officers and I hope they will come through this war safe and sound. Any of my pals can have what they wish of my things here.
>
> Goodbye & good luck to everyone.
>
> R A L Purves
>
> Quoted from *Those Who Fell in the Great War* National Archives of Scotland Reference SC70/8/418/2

To have chosen to say what they did on their son's inscription – At rest in peace – Robert Purves's parents must surely have known what he had done. But it's possible that no one else did. Mr and Mrs Purves entered their son's death in the Marquis de Ruvigny's *Biographical Record of all Members of His Majesty's Naval and Military Forces who have Fallen in the War* with the words:

> Joined the 9th Bttn The Royal Scots 6 Feb 1916: served with the Expeditionary Force in France and Flanders from 14 July, being attached to the 5th Bttn The Scottish Rifles, and was killed in action at Fricourt Wood, Mametz, 29 August following.

And when both parents were dead, one of their daughters included these words on their headstone in St Martin's New Burial Ground in Haddington, 'Also their son Robert who was killed in the Great War'.

DANZIG
ALLEY BRITISH
CEMTERY,
MAMETZ

AN AMERICAN CITIZEN

SECOND LIEUTENANT HARRY A BUTTERS
ROYAL FIELD ARTILLERY
DIED ON 31ST AUGUST 1916 AGED 24
BURIED IN MEAULTE MILITARY CEMETERY, FRANCE

American born, of English, Scottish, Irish and French ancestry, Harry Butters decided the moment war broke out that the Allied cause was just and that he was going to fight for it, regardless of America's strict policy of neutrality. He arrived in Britain early in 1915 and enlisted in the British Army. By September 1915 he was in France taking part in the Battle of Loos, after which he wrote:

> I find myself a soldier among millions of others in the great Allied Armies, fighting for all I believe to be right and civilized and humane against a power which is evil and which threatens the existence of all the rights we prize and the freedom we enjoy, although some of you in California as yet fail to realise it. ... but I tell you that not only am I willing to give my life to this enterprise ... but I firmly believe ... that never will I have an opportunity to gain so much honorable advancement for my own soul, or to do so much for the world's progress.

Ten days before his death, Butters wrote to the army chaplain saying, 'if I should happen to get wiped out' could you write to my sister as she has been 'mother, sister and everything else that is dear in the world to me'. Butter's parents were both dead. Butters also asked to be buried by the Roman Catholic padre if possible as this 'will give her greater consolation than anything – and please put after my name on the wooden cross – the bare fact that I was an American. I want this particularly, and I want her to know that it has been done so'. Two days later he was recalled to one of the batteries to replace a casualty and eight days after this he was dead. Whatever it said on his wooden cross, his headstone inscription reads, 'An American citizen'; he would be pleased. However, there could be a question as to whether he was still an American citizen. The United States had not yet come into the war and so to protect their neutrality soldiers who fought in foreign armies were technically no longer citizens. Despite the fact that he was a member of the British Army, Butters always maintained that he had not taken an oath of allegiance to the King and, although he is buried under a British headstone, his inscription ensures that his allegiance to America remains unquestioned.

Au revoir Llew

PRIVATE LLEWELLYN BRICK
DUKE OF WELLINGTON'S REGIMENT
DIED ON 3RD SEPTEMBER 1916 AGED 23
BURIED IN MILL ROAD CEMETERY, THIEPVAL, FRANCE

'Au revoir Llew', a simple farewell from a father in Yorkshire to his son buried in France, with the added poignancy that the father, Austin Brick, has expressed himself in French. Private Llewellyn Brick came from Lindley, a suburb of Huddersfield, Yorkshire. He and his family worked in the woollen industry: Llewellyn as a machine tenter – someone who stretched the newly dyed cloth over a frame to dry – Austin as a worsted worker, and sister Edith as a hank winder. Austin Brick originally came from Newtown, Montgomeryshire (Powys), which could explain his son's Welsh name. Llewellyn Brick was killed in the renewed British attack on Thiepval.

HE SAW BEYOND THE FILTH
OF BATTLE, AND THOUGHT DEATH
A FAIR PRICE TO PAY
TO BELONG TO THE COMPANY
OF THESE FELLOWS

SECOND LIEUTENANT WILLIAM ALEXANDER STANHOPE FORBES
DUKE OF CORNWALL'S LIGHT INFANTRY
DIED ON 3RD SEPTEMBER 1916 AGED 23
BURIED IN GUILLEMONT ROAD CEMETERY, GUILLEMONT, FRANCE

This beautiful inscription, with its Shakespearian resonances, was composed for his son by Stanhope Forbes RA. Although inscriptions were meant to be restricted to sixty-six characters this has ninety-one.

William Alexander Stanhope Forbes, known as Alec, was the only son of Stanhope and his first wife Elizabeth, both artists, who together founded the Newlyn School of Art. Alec, 21 when the war broke out, was initially declared unfit for military service. As a result he joined the Railway Operating Division as a Railway Transport Officer, eventually securing a transfer to the Duke of Cornwall's Light Infantry. He joined his regiment in France on 16 August 1916 and was killed eighteen days later leading his platoon in an attack on the village of Guillemont. The battalion war diary recorded that on the morning of 3 September, 'all ranks were full of confidence and in high spirits'. The regimental history takes the story on:

> The enemy met the advance with a very heavy barrage, but the Cornwall's pressed on steadily to their objective quite undeterred. Even the storm of machine gun fire brought to bear on them failed to stop them, for the German machine gun teams were soon disposed of by rifle-fire which showed the coolness and excellent marksmanship of the D.C.L.I.

Among the casualties of the action were 'four gallant young subalterns, all platoon commanders, who fell at the head of their men, killed or mortally wounded', among them Alec Forbes.

SECOND LIEUTENANT FORBES' HEADSTONE INSCRIPTION ON
HIS GRAVE IN GUILLEMONT ROAD CEMETERY

WE KNOW THAT HE ABIDETH IN US

CORPORAL EDWARD DWYER VC
EAST SURREY REGIMENT
DIED ON 3RD SEPTEMBER 1916 AGED 20
BURIED IN FLATIRON COPSE CEMETERY, MAMETZ, FRANCE

There is a note beside one of the inscriptions in the War Graves Commission's records, which states that, 'This headstone is to be engraved at the Commission's expense'. Why should this be? The man had no recorded next-of-kin, nor did plenty of soldiers, but what he did have was the Victoria Cross. His name was Edward Dwyer and at the time it was awarded he was the youngest recipient. Wounded soon after the incident, Dwyer was sent back to England to recover where, lionised by the public and the press, he became something of a celebrity.

Dwyer won his VC for 'most conspicuous bravery and devotion to duty at Hill 60 on 20th April, 1915', single-handedly fending off an enemy advance when the rest of his platoon were either dead or wounded. In an interview published in the *Daily Chronicle War Budget* on 8 July 1915, Dwyer, with typical British self-deprecation, says, 'They gave me the VC because I was in a dead funk at the idea of being taken prisoner by the Germans'. Dwyer's celebrity was undoubtedly used and promoted by the Government for recruiting purposes, and much of what he says in his interviews will have been suggested by them. However, it may have been Government propaganda but they are Dwyer's words: to the 'slackers' who grouse about the conditions they would have to put up with if they volunteered, 'I say that if the officers can put up with the grub and the grind, and men with money can serve as privates who've always lived soft before, nobody has any right to be too particular'.

Dwyer returned to the front, it is thought at his own request, and was killed in an attack on the German lines at Guillemont on 3 September 1916. His inscription, the Commission records do not say who chose it, comes from the First Epistle General of John Chapter 3, verse 24:

> And he that keepeth His commandments dwelleth in Him, and He in him. And thereby we know that He abideth in us, by the spirit which He hath given us.

ONE GIFT HE HAD
ONE ROYAL GIFT HE GAVE

CAPTAIN ARNOLD MCLINTOCK
DUKE OF WELLINGTON'S WEST RIDING REGIMENT
DIED ON 3RD SEPTEMBER 1916 AGED 31
BURIED IN TO MILL ROAD CEMETERY, THIEPVAL, FRANCE

The 3 September 1916 was a black day for the West Riding of Yorkshire when the 49th (West Riding) Division went into action at Thiepval with very heavy casualties. The men of the 1st/5th Battalion, of which Captain McLintock was a Company Commander, came from the Huddersfield, Meltham area where McLintock was a partner in his uncle's woollen mill and where many of the men worked in the business. Of the 450 men who went into the attack, 350 became casualties, 106 of them killed. Captain McLintock, described as Lieutenant McLintock in the War Diary, led 'A' Company in an assault on the Pope's Nose. It's difficult to determine exactly what happened, but although there were reports that the German front line had been taken, the positions could not be held. Mary McLintock, Arnold's mother, chose his inscription – 'One gift he had, one royal gift he gave'. The words come from a longer passage that is sometimes found as a dedication on war memorials but never with any attribution. The gift that McLintock and so many others gave was, of course, their lives, their futures.

> Ever for him life's brilliant banners wave,
> Borne on the breeze of man's courageous spell.
> He shall not know the weary bitterness
> That haunts me still, he slumbers but too well.
> One gift he had, one royal gift he gave
> A gift that meant for him the summer sun,
> Youth's glorious hopes; the lover's ecstasy,
> Life's fair adventure scarcely yet begun.
> One gift he had, one royal gift he gave
> Proud to exchange it for a soldier's grave.

BRIGHT, INTELLIGENT LAD WAS RESPECTED & LOVED BY ALL HIS REGIMENT

LANCE CORPORAL SYDNEY JAMES ARMSTRONG SAWYERS
AUSTRALIAN INFANTRY
DIED ON 7TH SEPTEMBER 1916 AGED 24
BURIED IN CONTAY BRITISH CEMETERY, FRANCE

This inscription sounds very much as though it comes from a letter of condolence from the soldier's senior officer to his parents; it has that formal yet consoling tone. British officers must have written many hundreds of letters of condolence during the war. Every single family of every soldier killed will have received at least one, and sometimes more than one. And that was in addition to the formal telegram – in the case of officers – and letter – in the case of soldiers, and the letter from the King and Queen. The fact that these letters did bring consolation is evident from the extracts that appear in personal inscriptions, like Sawyers'. Sawyers was a photographer. His family lived in Norseman Western Australia, a gold mining town. He enlisted on 5 July 1915, embarked for Europe on 1 October that year and died of wounds just under a year later on 7 September 1915 at No. 49 Casualty Clearing Station, Contay.

Lepaa rauhassa rakastettu ja kaivattu

SAPPER ANDREW MYLLYMAKI
CANADIAN ENGINEERS
DIED ON 9TH SEPTEMBER 1916 AGED 26
BURIED IN ALBERT COMMUNAL CEMETERY EXTENSION, FRANCE

Andrew Myllymaki's inscription is in Finnish and means 'Rest in peace beloved, deeply missed'. His brother, who he had named as his next-of-kin, chose it for him. Sapper Myllymaki was born in Canada to Finnish parents. They were among the many Finns who emigrated to Canada in the later part of the 19th Century, driven from Finland by the increasing Russianisation of the country and lured to Canada by the plentiful opportunities it offered, especially in the copper mines. Andrew Myllymaki was born in White Fish, Ontario but his parents soon moved to settle in New Finland in Saskatchewan. He was studying Engineering at Queen's University, Ontario when the war broke out and enlisted almost straightaway, early in September 1914. He served with the Canadian 1st Division Engineers who arrived in France in February 1915. Having spent the early summer of 1916 in the Ypres region, they moved to the Somme in late August in preparation for the attack on Courcellette. He died on 9 September 1916, a day when the 1st Division were in action at Pozieres.

O SO YOUNG & YET SO BRAVE

PRIVATE JAMES RATHBAND
ROYAL DUBLIN FUSILIERS
DIED ON 9TH SEPTEMBER 1916 AGED 16
BURIED IN DELVILLE WOOD CEMETERY, LONGUEVAL, FRANCE

Private James Rathband was 16 when he was killed in action at the capture of Ginchy on 9 September 1916. This was the same action in which the Irish journalist, Home Rule politician and barrister, Tom Kettle, serving in the same battalion, was also killed. James Rathband has not left any written record of his experiences but in a way Captain Tom Kettle has done it for him. This letter to Kettle's brother was written on the day before the battle:

> We are moving up tonight into the battle of the Somme. The bombardment, destruction and bloodshed are beyond all imagination, nor did I ever think the valour of simple men could be quite as beautiful as that of my Dublin Fusiliers. ... The big guns are coughing and smacking their shells, which sound for all the world like over-head express trains, at anything from 10 to 100 per minute on this sector; ... Somewhere the Choosers of the Slain are touching, as in our Norse stories they used to touch, with invisible wands those who are to die.

The 'Choosers' chose both Tom Kettle and James Rathband together with sixty-one other men of the 9th Battalion on that day.

The son of Joseph and Annie Rathband of Dublin, James's inscription was signed for by his sister Annie, Miss A Rathband, 12E Abbey Cottages, Upper Abbey Street, Dublin, a street of very modest, back-to-back terraced houses that no longer exist. Where did the inscription come from? Had Annie Rathband read it somewhere? Put the words into *Google* and they come up in at least three nineteenth-century romantic novels to describe young heroes whose deeds belied their years – just as James Rathband's must have done.

ELSKET OG SAVNET
AF MODER OG SOSKENDE

LANCE SERJEANT JORGEN KORNERUP BANG
ROYAL FUSILIERS
DIED ON 10TH SEPTEMBER 1916 AGED 30
BURIED IN BERTRANCOURT MILITARY CEMETERY, FRANCE

Jorgen Kornerop Bang was a Dane, a master builder from Silkeborg in Northern Jutland, a Danish national athlete, the winner of fourteen Danish decathlon championships and the holder of nine Danish javelin records who died serving as a Lance Serjeant in the British Army. Denmark was neutral in the First World War, a position she maintained with some difficulty. Many Danes still felt a residual hostility towards Germany over her annexation of Schleswigh-Holstein in 1864. But mindful of Belgium's fate, Denmark was keen not to give Germany any reason to invade. Denmark mobilized her reserves, 50,000 men, to defend her borders, whilst Germany called up the young men of Schleswig-Holstein to fight for the Fatherland. A small number of Danes, it's estimated to be in the region of about eighty-five, joined the French Army. It's not known how many joined the British but Jorgen Kornerop Bang must have been one of them. He served with the 17th Battalion the Royal Fusiliers, the City of London Regiment, who made use of his javelin skills by putting him in charge of grenade-throwing training. Unfortunately he was killed when a grenade exploded prematurely. Kornerop Bang's inscription is in Danish. It means, 'Loved and missed by mother and siblings'. It is said that one of his brothers, Johannes, also served in the British Army and died at Verdun on 12 October 1918. However, none of Jorgen's siblings were called Johannes, there isn't a Johannes Kornerop Bang in the War Graves Commission registers and if there were he wouldn't have died at Verdun since that is the one place where the French always fought on their own. It's possible that Johannes was a cousin, one of the eighty-five Danes who volunteered to fight in the French Army.

Rest in the Lord
& wait patiently for Him

SERJEANT WILLIAM ECCLES HOLT
KING'S OWN ROYAL LANCASTER REGIMENT
DIED ON 10TH SEPTEMBER 1916 AGED 39
BURIED IN DELVILLE WOOD CEMETERY, LONGUEVAL, FRANCE

Serjeant Holt's widow chose his inscription, which quotes Psalm 37 verse 7: 'Rest in the Lord, and wait patiently for him: fret not thyself because of him who prospereth in his way, because of the man who bringeth wicked devices to pass'. The words form the opening lines of a beautiful aria from Mendelssohn's *Elijah*:

> O rest in the Lord, wait patiently for Him,
> And he shall give thee thy heart's desires.
> Commit thy way unto Him, and trust in Him,
> And fret not thyself because of evil doers.

Holt had already served twelve years with the army before the First World War broke out. In 1897, when he was 18, he had enlisted with the Royal North Lancashire Fusiliers and served with them in South Africa during the Boer War being present at the relief of Kimberley. He retired — time expired — in 1909. On the outbreak war in 1914, he joined the King's Own Royal Lancaster Regiment and went with them to France in February 1915. Holt survived the fighting of First Ypres and both Delville and High Wood but was killed on the morning of 10 September by a shell, which exploded among the working party he was bringing in from a night's work in the trenches. A married man and the father of two daughters, his son was born eight weeks after his death. He was baptized William Eccles Holt.

Joined His Majesty's Forces August 31st 1914 Proceeded to France January 1915

CORPORAL DONALD HUME NODING
LONDON REGIMENT, QUEEN'S WESTMINSTER RIFLES
DIED ON 10TH SEPTEMBER 1916 AGED 21
BURIED IN COMBLES COMMUNAL CEMETERY EXTENSION, FRANCE

On Monday 31 August 1914 more men joined the British Army than on any one single day since the war had begun. Why ... because on Sunday the 30th a special edition of *The Times* had published the Amiens Dispatch. Ten days after the first engagement with the enemy the British public finally learnt how things really stood. In those ten days the army had fallen back from Namur and Mons and was now fighting not in Belgium but in France with General French talking about the need to defend Le Havre 210 miles away on the French coast.

The British public knew nothing of this. By Thursday the 27th all *The Times* could say was: 'Though we know the British Army acquitted itself with distinction at Mons, we know very little more'. And on Friday the 28th: 'Our Army was heavily engaged yesterday in co-operation with the French against superior numbers, and once more it splendidly sustained its fighting reputation'. But by Saturday it was hinting: 'Our soldiers fought as men of the British race have ever fought, but it would serve no useful purpose now to hide the heaviness of the price of their bravery'.

The Government was in turmoil, would the truth be bad for morale or a boost to recruitment? *The Times* was of the opinion that it would boost recruitment so, with some unofficial encouragement, which was quickly denied, it published the dispatch it had just received from Amiens. This told 'a bitter tale' of a 'retreating and broken army', with 'grievously injured regiments'.

The report produced the predictable uproar and the paper was accused of irresponsible sensationalism. But the next day recruitment increased and by the end of the week 174,901 men had enlisted compared with the 100,000 that had done so in the previous eighteen days. Noding's inscription, confirmed by his mother, expressed the family's pride in the fact that he had been among these early volunteers.

HE TAKING DEATH ON HIMSELF
SAVED HIS COMRADES

CORPORAL GERALD EDMOND PATTINSON
MACHINE GUN CORPS (HEAVY BRANCH)
DIED ON 15TH SEPTEMBER 1916 AGED 31
BURIED IN COMBLES COMMUNAL CEMETERY EXTENSION

The British Army used tanks in battle for the very first time at Flers-Courcelette on 15 September 1916. Corporal Pattinson was a member of the crew of tank C14 under the command of Second Lieutenant Francis Arnold. C14 took part in the attack on Bouleaux Wood but after using its machine guns to good effect it ditched in a shell hole. Pattinson with three other members of the crew attempted to dig it out but came under attack from German grenade throwers. A grenade fell among the group and Pattinson picked it up to throw it back but it exploded and killed him. This is the action behind his inscription. The Pattinson family must have had a difficult war: Mrs Pattinson was a German citizen born in Hamburg in 1851 and certainly at the time of the 1911 census they had a German domestic servant in the household.

Although the War Graves Commission has his names as Gerald Edmonds, from the census it looks as though his second name was Edmond.

HE DIED THE NOBLEST DEATH
A MAN MAY DIE
FIGHTING FOR GOD & RIGHT
& LIBERTY

LIEUTENANT ARTHUR STANLEY CAREY
MIDDLESEX REGIMENT
DIED ON 15TH SEPTEMBER 1916 AGED 25
BURIED IN COMBLES COMMUNAL CEMETERY EXTENSION, FRANCE

Carey's inscription comes from *To You Who Have Lost* by John Oxenham, printed in his popular book of verse, *All's Well,* which was published in 1915. The lines regularly appear in personal inscriptions and as a dedication on war memorials. The first verse reads:

> I know! I know! –
> The ceaseless ache, the emptiness the woe, –
> The pang of loss, –
> The strength that sinks beneath so sore a cross.
> " – Heedless and careless, still the world wags on,
> And leaves me broken ... Oh, my son! my son!"
> Yet – think of this! –
> Yes, rather think on this! –
> He died as few men get the chance to die
> Fighting to save a world's morality.
> He died the noblest death a man may die,
> Fighting for God, and Right, and Liberty; –
> And such a death is Immortality.

Arthur Carey was the son of a laundry manager in Brixton, London. His father made a point of outlining his son's education in the War Graves Commission's cemetery register: 'Educated in Hanover, at the Lycee Lakanal, Paris, and at the Strand School, London, where he won the Grand Concours Medal for French 1911'. By implication, Arthur Carey was tri-lingual. In the 1911 census he was working as a bank clerk. He served with the 1st/8th Battalion Middlesex Regiment, and was killed in action on 15 September when the Battalion was brought up in support of the 7th Battalion, which had attacked at Bouleaux Wood.

SMALL TIME BUT IN THAT SMALL MOST GREATLY LIVED THIS STAR OF ENGLAND

LIEUTENANT RAYMOND ASQUITH
GRENADIER GUARDS
DIED ON 15TH SEPTEMBER 1916 AGED 37
BURIED IN GUILLEMONT ROAD CEMETERY, GUILLEMONT, FRANCE

> We greatly regret to record the death in action on September 15th of Lieutenant Raymond Asquith, Grenadier Guards, by which the Prime Minister loses his eldest son and the country a man of brilliant promise.
> *The Times*, September 19th 1916

This epitaph comes from the epilogue to Shakespeare's *Henry V*, and was chosen by Raymond's wife, Katherine. It is often said that Raymond was one of the most brilliant men killed in the war. He was brilliant but never ambitious for his brilliance. As his friend John Buchan put it, Raymond had about him 'the suggestion of some urbane and debonair scholar-gipsy, who belonged to a different world from the rest of us'. In addition, 'he scorned the worldly wisdom which makes smooth the steps in a career'. On 15 September 1916, the Guards attacked at Lesboeufs. John Buchan later wrote that, 'Their front of attack was too narrow, their objectives were too far distant, and from the start their flanks were enfiladed'. Raymond was shot in the chest as he led his Company into a hail of bullets. He was taken to the dressing station where he died but not before he had put on a magnificent show of nonchalance, smoking a cigarette to disguise the extent of his injuries, and asking the medical orderly if he would send his flask on to his father. Margot Asquith, Raymond's stepmother, broke the news to her husband the Prime Minister Herbert Henry Asquith who, 'put his head on his arms on the table and sobbed passionately'. Later Asquith wrote that, 'Counsellors tell me that I ought not to be sorrowful. But I am: like a man out of whose sky the twin stars of Pride and Hope have both vanished into lasting darkness'. 'Twin stars', 'this star of England', the same stellar image occurred to both father and wife. And the father, who had apparently never written to his son once whilst he was at the front, is said to have kept his son's flask beside his bed for the rest of his life.

LIEUTENANT
RAYMOND ASQUITH
GRENADIER GUARDS
15TH SEPTEMBER 1916 AGE 37

ALL TIME BUT IN THAT SMALL
MOST GREATLY LIVED
STORY OF ENGLAND

**LIEUTENANT
ASQUITH'S
HEADSTONE IN
GUILLEMONT ROAD
CEMETERY**

ONE CLEAR CALL

LIEUTENANT SIDNEY MAURICE SCOTT
COLDSTREAM GUARDS
DIED ON 15TH SEPTEMBER 1916 AGED 19
BURIED IN GUARDS' CEMETERY, LESBOEUFS, FRANCE

Sidney Scott's widowed mother chose his inscription, a quotation from Alfred, Lord Tennyson's *Crossing the Bar*, which reflects the poet's quiet acceptance of his own approaching death.

> Sunset and evening star,
> And one clear call for me!
> And may there be no moaning at the bar,
> When I put out to sea,
>
> But such a tide as moving seems asleep,
> Too full for sound and foam,
> When that which drew from out the boundless deep
> Turns again home.
>
> Twilight and evening bell,
> And after that the dark!
> And may there be no sadness of farewell,
> When I embark;
>
> For tho' from out our bourne of Time and Place
> The flood may bear me far,
> I hope to see my Pilot face to face
> When I have crossed the bar.

Scott's brother, Second Lieutenant Basil John Harrison Scott, had been killed in action at Ypres on 23 October 1914. He is commemorated on the Menin Gate.

PEACE WAS THE PRIZE
OF ALL HIS TOIL AND CARE

CAPTAIN DAVID HENDERSON
MIDDLESEX REGIMENT
DIED ON 15TH SEPTEMBER 1916 AGED 27
BURIED IN LONDON CEMETERY AND EXTENSION, LONGUEVILLE, FRANCE

Captain David Henderson was the eldest son of the Rt. Hon. Arthur Henderson MP, a leading Trade Unionist, Labour politician and Labour member of Asquith's Coalition Government. David Henderson too was a Trade Unionist; he was a member of the British Steel Smelters' Union and worked in the office of John Hodge, the Labour MP for Manchester, Gorton.

Arthur Henderson had initially opposed the war, but once Britain was committed he supported it. His son, David, enlisted a month after the outbreak in September 1914, was gazetted Second Lieutenant in February 1915 and obtained his captaincy that June. He was killed in action on the same day as the Prime Minister's son, Raymond Asquith.

David Henderson's inscription comes from verse 16 of *A Poem upon the Death of His Late Highness, Oliver, Lord Protector of England, Scotland, and Ireland* by John Dryden, 1631-1700.

> Peace was the Prize of all his Toil and Care,
> Which War had banish'd and did now restore

Cromwell was admired by the Labour Party for his radical politics but was still a controversial figure at the beginning of the twentieth century because of his republicanism and his suppression of Ireland.

In supporting the war, David's father, Arthur Henderson, had not only wanted a British victory but a just and democratic peace. As Labour Foreign Secretary, 1929-1931, he supported the League of Nations, sought the resolution of international incidents by diplomatic means and worked hard to support the peace his son's death had bought. Arthur Henderson was awarded the Nobel Prize for Peace in 1934: 'Peace was the prize of all his toil and care'.

OF PHILADELPHIA, U.S.A.

LIEUTENANT DILLWYN PARRISH STARR
COLDSTREAM GUARDS
DIED ON 15TH SEPTEMBER 1916 AGED 32
BURIED IN GUARDS' CEMETERY LESBOEUFS, FRANCE

Dillwyn Starr's father, in recording that his son came from Philadelphia, USA, flags up the fact that Dillwyn was an American citizen and that he was a member of the socially prominent Philadelphian Starr family.

Dillwyn was a charmingly charismatic figure who never really settled to anything before the war broke out whereupon his sense of adventure immediately drew him to the action. Many Americans were furious and ashamed by President Wilson's attitude to the war and openly did what they could to aid the Allied war effort. Many British people were furious too and Dillwyn wrote how he was 'constantly in hot-water about home, as all here know I am an American'.

The regiment embarked for France on 11 July 1916, ten days after the launch of the Somme offensive. On 15 September the Guards attacked at Lesboeufs. Dillwyn knew the attack was coming and told his parents, 'They hope here that we shall break through the German lines, but I have my doubts'. Eight days later the Guards did capture Lesboeufs but by then Dillwyn was dead, killed as he led his platoon across No-Mans-Land against 'a perfect storm of shells and a hail of machine gun bullets'. They reached the German trenches where 'Dillwyn fell, just as he was springing upon its parapet, with his face to the enemy, shot through the heart and killed instantly'.

Dillwyn's parents received numerous letters of condolence many, like the one below, expressing their gratitude for what Dillwyn, an American had done.

> You must be proud to have a son who died so nobly fighting not for
> his country but what must be accounted far higher, for the cause of
> Humanity and on the side of God. If we regard our own countrymen
> as heroes he is far more. America may be proud to rear such men.

LIEUTENANT STARR'S
HEADSTONE IN
GUARDS' CEMETERY,
LESBOEUFS

GRENADE THROWER
DIED AS A SOLDIER
AT HIS POST

PRIVATE JOHN DUNCAN MACPHERSON
SCOTS GUARDS
DIED ON 15TH SEPTEMBER 1916 AGED 21
BURIED IN GUARDS' CEMETERY LESBOEUFS, FRANCE

This inscription, which was chosen by Private Macpherson's father, has to be the ultimate accolade for a soldier, implying as it does the faithful discharge of duty regardless of cost. Macpherson served with the 1st Battalion Scots Guards, which took part in the Guards' Division attack at Ginchy on 15 September. This was the day that Lance-Serjeant Frederick McNess, who like Macpherson was in the 1st Battalion, won a Victoria Cross 'during a severe engagement' and 'in the face of heavy shell and machine gun fire'. At the end of the day, the 1st Battalion had lost thirty-eight dead, a number that rose to eighty-three when all the missing were accounted for. As a grenade thrower, Private Macpherson would have been a member of a nine-man team consisting of an NCO, two grenade throwers, two carriers, two bayonet men to protect the team and two spare men in case of casualties. When the attack reached the enemy trenches the grenade throwers' task was to rush along them lobbing grenades into dugouts so as to kill the occupants still sheltering there before they could emerge and fight back.

HE DID HIS BEST
GOD GRANT HIM ETERNAL REST
DAD, MAM, EDGAR

GUARDSMAN WILLIAM JOHN WILLIAMS
RIFLE BRIGADE
DIED ON 15TH SEPTEMBER 1916 AGED 21
BURIED IN GUARDS' CEMETERY LESBOEUFS, FRANCE

Guardsman Williams' inscription is interesting because of the documentation surrounding it that survives in the Imperial War Museum. In her book *Grief in Wartime*, Carol Acton relates how, ten years after William John Williams' death, his family – the Dad, Mam and Edgar who are named in the inscription – visit his grave, an event they later describe in a letter to a Miss O'Neill who appears to have been William John's girlfriend.

> And it was very easy to find the grave of our Dear William John, as we were going from the entrance ... there stood his name, his rank, regiment and no 13369 quite clear, and every letter correct, as we wish to inscribe on his tombstone ... Now came the burst of tears, but with a hope to meet our dear, brave lad again in a far and better sphear (sic) than this world, where there is no sorrow, nor tears, nor cruel wars, where we shall enjoy everlasting life, when God will wipe every tear. We parted from the Cemetary (sic), very much satisfied and lot better after we seen (sic) his lasting resting place and see the care is taken by our Government of the Cemetary (sic)."

The family left a wreath on his grave, which was signed:

> Father, Mother, Brother, Miss Annie O'Neill
> A silent thought, a secret tear

Ten years after their son's death his parents have been able to weep over his grave and this, together with the respectful way in which the cemetery is maintained, brings them great comfort.

AWAKE AND SING
YE THAT DWELL IN DUST

CAPTAIN ARTHUR INNES ADAM
CAMBRIDGESHIRE REGIMENT
DIED ON 16TH SEPTEMBER 1916 AGED 22
BURIED IN ACHIET-LE-GRAND COMMUNAL CEMETERY EXTENSION, FRANCE

Thy dead men shall live, together with my dead body shall they arise.
Awake and sing, ye that dwell in dust: Isaiah 26:19

Four years after her son went missing, Mrs Adela Marion Adam was forced to conclude that, as 'Exhaustive enquiries in Germany, and through several neutral countries and America, have failed to discover the least vestige' of his fate, 'there is no glimmer to lighten the impenetrable darkness'. Adam was killed because he accompanied a platoon on a raid when he shouldn't have done.

> Under the scheme for the attack Shaw was to be the only officer with the party; but they were all mere lads, and who could blame one so young and fearless for desiring to be with those he commanded in their hour of danger? He had worked for his men day in and day out, and loved them all. As a soldier he was wrong, but as a man he felt he could not leave them.
> *The Cambridgeshires 1914-1919*, Riddell and Clayton 1934

In September 1920, Adam's body was located in a German cemetery at Achiet-le-Petit, and in 1924 it was reinterred in Achiet-le-Grand.

Arthur Innes Adam was a prize-winning scholar at Winchester and Balliol College, Oxford, but as his mother was forced to conclude, 'It is idle to enquire what he might have become; let us sing *Laus Deo* for what he was'. However, we might allow ourselves a little speculation. On 2 November 1915 Adam wrote to his sister, Barbara, saying that for the last two years he had had 'a kind of hope in him' that some day they might be able to work together towards lessening the misery caused by wrong-doing. And that 'at least, if I am killed, I will now have mentioned the idea to you ...'. In 1958, his sister, the economist and social scientist Barbara Wootton, 'an acknowledged expert in criminology, penology, and social work' [Oxford DNB], was created Baroness Wootton of Abinger for her work in these areas. What might she and her brother have done together?

He is not dead
He hath awakened
From the dream of life

LIEUTENANT FRANCIS ARTHUR RALFS
ROYAL FUSILIERS
DIED ON 16TH SEPTEMBER 1916 AGED 22
BURIED IN PUCHEVILLERS BRITISH CEMETERY, FRANCE

Francis Ralfs' inscription comes from stanza XXXIX of Percy Bysshe Shelley's *Adonais: an Elegy on the Death of John Keats*, 1821.

> Peace, peace! he is not dead, he doth not sleep,
> He hath awaken'd from the dream of life;
> ... We decay
> Like corpses in a charnel; fear and grief
> Convulse us and consume us day by day,
> And cold hopes swarm like worms within our living clay.

The poem is an obvious source of comfort for those mourning young men dead before their time: they will not grow old as we shall, fear and grief will not touch them any more. An obvious source of comfort? This is what Cynthia Asquith has to say about the death of her brother, Yvo Charteris:

> Somehow with the others who have been killed, I have acutely felt the
> loss of them but have so swallowed the rather high-faluting platitude
> that it was all right for them – that they were not to be pitied, but were
> safe, unassailable, young and glamorous for ever. With Yvo – I can't
> bear it for him. The sheer pity and horror of it is overwhelming and I
> am haunted by the feeling that he is disappointed.

At the time of his death Ralfs was attached to the Lancashire Fusiliers. He died on 16 September of wounds received on the 12th, when part of a trenching party.

> Digging at Authuille Wood. Lieutenant F.A. Ralfs wounded (died of
> wounds); one other rank killed one wounded.
> Battalion War Diary 12 September 1916

THEY SHALL BE MINE
SAITH THE LORD
THAT DAY
WHEN I MAKE UP MY JEWELS

CAPTAIN MARK TENNANT
SCOTS GUARDS
DIED ON 16TH SEPTEMBER 1916 AGED 24
BURIED IN GUARDS' CEMETERY LESBOEUFS, FRANCE

> And they shall be mine, saith the Lord of hosts, in that day when I
> make up my jewels; and I will spare them, as a man spareth his own
> son that serveth him. *Malachi* 3: 16-17

These words from the Old Testament form the basis of a once well-known children's hymn, *When he Cometh*, which was popular with soldiers too:

> He will gather, He will gather
> The gems for His kingdom;
> All the pure ones, all the bright ones,
> His loved and his own.

In his autobiography, *Drawn from Memory*, Ernest Shepard recalled hearing it 'sung by Welsh voices on a dusty shell-torn road in Picardy, as a battalion of Welch Fusiliers marched into battle'. Mark was killed the day after the Guards' attack at Lesboeufs, as Cynthia Asquith reported:

> He had got through the battle all right, and had gone across to another
> trench to congratulate his brother-in-law, Ian Colquhoun, on both their
> escapes; on his way back, Ian saw him blown to bits by a stray shell.

In 1920, Mark's youngest brother, John Tennant, dedicated his wartime memoir, *In the Clouds Above Baghdad,* to his brother Mark, commenting in the foreword, 'life is respectable and comfortable – and safe. The majority of us who have survived this war are no doubt doomed to die in our beds; when that moment arrives how we shall envy that gay company who went before, sword in hand and faces to the enemy, flower of a generation'.

John Tennant was killed on 7 August 1941 whilst on active service during the Second World War when the starboard engine on his aircraft failed during a flying training flight. He was 51.

Sans peur et sans reproche

SERJEANT JOHN STONE HEPWORTH MM
DUKE OF WELLINGTON'S WEST RIDING REGIMENT
DIED ON 22ND SEPTEMBER 1916 AGED 25
BURIED IN BLIGHTY VALLEY CEMETERY, AUTHUILLE WOOD, FRANCE

The phrase translates as fearless and faultless but it resonates with associations that date back to the Age of Chivalry. 'Chevalier sans peur et sans reproche' was the tribute attached to Pierre Terrail (1473-1524), the Chevalier Bayard, who, according to the chroniclers, was the epitome of chivalry: a brave and skillful commander and a fair and honourable foe. Association with Bayard implied piety, generosity, honour, independence, truthfulness, loyalty, courtesy, modesty, humanity and respect for women, as enumerated by Kenelm Digby in his *Broad-Stone of Honour or Rules for the Gentlemen of England*, published in 1822. The story of Bayard was given a further boost with the publication in 1911 of Christopher Hare's *The Good Knight Without Fear Without Reproach*.

To be associated with Bayard was a great compliment whether one was the English general Sir James Outram, hero of the Indian Mutiny, buried in Westminster Abbey under a slab inscribed with the words 'The Bayard of India', or John Hepworth, a serjeant in the Duke of Westminster's West Riding Regiment killed on the Somme during the First World War.

IF THIS IS VICTORY, THEN LET GOD STOP ALL WARS HIS LOVING MOTHER

PRIVATE FRANK HITCHIN
MACHINE GUN CORPS
DIED ON 22ND SEPTEMBER 1916 AGED 18
BURIED IN GROVE TOWN CEMETERY, MEAULTE, FRANCE

Frank Hitchin died at a Casualty Clearing Station at Meaulte on 22 September. Serving with the 59th Battalion Machine Gun Corps, part of the 12th Division, he could have been injured in any of their Somme battles: Delville Wood (15 July-3 September), Guillemont (3 September-6 September) or Flers-Courcelette (15 September-22 September).

This is an interesting inscription. There is no suggestion that the cost of victory has been worth it, quite the contrary. Here victory is not associated with Christ's triumph over death, there is no suggestion that 'Death is swallowed up in victory', no scorning of the reality of its finality, 'O death where is thy sting? O grave where is thy victory?' (1 Corinthians 15:54 & 55).

Mrs Martha Williamson chose her son's inscription. He is buried in a cemetery along with 1,390 other young men, in one of many hundreds of cemeteries along the Western Front. Her meaning is clear, what is the point of a victory that has killed so many.

The War Graves Commission had given itself the right to censor inscriptions, and it did: 'His loving parents curse the Hun'; 'He died the just for the unjust'; 'Set out to save England. Result: England permanently damned'. These are some of the inscriptions it would not allow. Insulting the Germans by calling them Huns, or the unjust, was not allowed, nor did the Commission want you to imply that Britain had been harmed by the war. Suggesting that it had all been a huge waste must have come close.

KILLED IN ACTION
IN HIS TWENTIETH YEAR

LIEUTENANT THE HON. EDWARD WYNDHAM TENNANT
GRENADIER GUARDS
DIED ON 22ND SEPTEMBER 1916 AGED 19
BURIED IN GUILLEMONT ROAD CEMETERY, GUILLEMONT, FRANCE

This is a simple inscription that nevertheless says much about the mindset of the soldier's parents. Born on 1 August 1897, Edward Tennant was 19 and three months when he died. He had joined up on the outbreak of war when he was just 17, and had been at the front since he was eighteen. No soldier was allowed to serve overseas until he was nineteen, unless he had his parents' permission. In her son's memoir, Lady Glenconner explains his presence at the front: 'On account of his efficiency as an officer he had the honour of being especially selected to go out to France, although Brigade Orders had just been issued that no one should leave England before nineteen years of age'. Presumably she and her husband had also given their permission. Many of the first volunteers were as young as Tennant, and many of their parents felt angry with the Government because it had delayed introducing conscription until January 1916. This delay meant that it was their young sons who bore the brunt of the fighting, and their young sons who were dying. The inscription they chose suggests that the Glenconners felt this way too. Edward wrote a moving letter to his mother on the eve of battle, published in Laurence Weaver's *War Letters of Fallen Englishmen*. Brief extracts illustrate his mind:

> ... tomorrow we go over the top ... I am full of hope and trust, and pray that I may be worthy of my fighting ancestors ... I feel rather like saying 'If it be possible let this cup pass from me,' but the triumphant finish 'nevertheless not what I will but what Thou willest,' steels my heart and sends me into this battle with a heart of triple bronze ... Brutus' farewell to Cassius sounds in my heart: 'If not farewell; and if we meet again, we shall smile'.

Edward was killed by a sniper two days later. According to the battalion history:

> ... the Hon. E.W. Tennant, who had been left in Gas Alley, had occupied his time shooting at the enemy. Apparently there was some movement by the Germans which led him to shoot with his revolver, and a moment later he fell dead, shot through the head by one of the enemy's snipers.

GUILLEMONT ROAD
CEMETERY

Thou called me to resign
What most I prized
He ne'er was mine

SECOND LIEUTENANT TERENCE WILLIAM HONYCHURCH
MIDDLESEX REGIMENT
DIED ON 22ND SEPTEMBER 1916 AGED 21
BURIED IN GROVE TOWN CEMETERY, MEAULTE, FRANCE

> If Thou should'st call me to resign
> What most I prize, - it ne'er was mine;
> I only yield Thee what was Thine; —
> "Thy will be done."

Terence Honychurch's inscription comes from the hymn *My God My Father While I Stray*. Can you see the difference between the verse from the hymn and Honychurch's inscription? There is no 'if' about the epitaph and no 'it' about what was most prized. God did call Second Lieutenant Honychurch's widowed mother to relinquish what she most prized and 'he' was her son. Charles Wesley wrote the hymn from which the inscription comes, each of its seven verses acknowledging that whatever hardships God throws in life's way, his will should be accepted — 'Thy will be done'.

> Renew my will from day to day,
> Blend it with Thine, and take away
> All that now makes it hard to say,
> "Thy will be done."

Mrs Honychurch was the widow of a clothier's outfitter. She had a daughter, Elsie, who in 1911 was a pupil at the Warehousemen, Clerks and Drapers' Orphan School in Purley, Surrey. Fifteen-year-old Terence was a draper's apprentice in Stroud. Perhaps he too had been a pupil at the school. Terence Honychurch served with the 1st/7th Middlesex Regiment and was attached to 167 Trench Mortar Battery, part of the 56th London Division. He died of wounds in a Casualty Clearing Station at Meaulte on 22 September 1916.

THE PURPOSES OF LIFE MISUNDERSTOOD

PRIVATE CHARLES DOYLE
ROYAL ARMY MEDICAL CORPS
DIED ON 24TH SEPTEMBER 1916 AGED 22
BURIED IN GUARDS' CEMETERY LESBOEUFS, FRANCE

Mrs Elizabeth Doyle, Charles Doyle's mother, makes no attempt to wrap her son's death in religious, patriotic or chivalric language. To her, life is for living, not killing. Given the chance to express herself publicly, even if only on his headstone, her response to her son's death is uncompromising - 'the purposes of life misunderstood'. Mrs Doyle had two reasons to be unimpressed by the war, her husband Charles Edward Doyle had volunteered to fight, despite being beyond the age of military service, and had been killed in Mesopotamia just five months before her son.

Charles Doyle served with the Royal Army Medical Corps and in September 1916 was a member of the 18th Field Ambulance unit attached to the 6th Division. On the 21 September they went into the trenches at Morval on the Somme and on the 24th the unit's war diary recorded, 'one of our stretcher bearers killed by a shell & one wounded by shrapnel'. The dead stretcher bearer was Charles Doyle.

His father, Charles Edward Doyle, was a serjeant in the 6th Battalion the Loyal North Lancashire Regiment, part of the 13th Division. He served with it in Gallipoli and then in Mesopotamia where he was killed on 9 April at Sanna-i-Yat. Doyle may originally have had a grave but he doesn't now and is commemorated on the Basra Memorial. He was 42.

Mrs Doyle hadn't always expressed herself in this negative manner over her son's death. On 18 October 1916 the following announcement appeared in the *Manchester Evening News*:

DOYLE C – In loving memory of my dear son Private C Doyle 20001 RAMC who fell in action September 24 1916 Mother, sisters, brothers. A good life is often too short but a good name endureth for ever

Sleep after toil
Port after stormy seas
Ease after war

CAPTAIN OSWALD ALEXANDER HERD
DURHAM LIGHT INFANTRY
DIED ON 24TH SEPTEMBER 1916 AGED 25
BURIED IN GUARDS' CEMETERY LESBOEUFS, FRANCE

On 21 September 1916, the 14th Battalion Durham Light Infantry went into the trenches near Guillemont between Trones and Bernafray woods. Here they came under heavy and sustained German artillery fire until the morning of the 24th when the Germans launched an infantry attack on their trenches. The Germans were driven back and the British guns opened up in retaliation. Unfortunately the British shells fell short and one dropped into a 14th Battalion trench killing Herd and three other soldiers. Captain Herd's mother, Constance Herd, confirmed his inscription, a quotation from Edmund Spenser's *Fairie Queen*.

> Is not short pain well born, that brings long ease,
> And lays the Soul to sleep in quiet grave?
> Sleep after toil, port after stormy seas,
> Ease after war, death after life, does greatly please.
> > Edmund Spenser 1552-1599
> > *The Fairie Queen*: Book 1 Canto IX

IN SHORT MEASURES
LIFE MAY PERFECT BE

LIEUTENANT DOUGLAS OLIPHANT CONSTABLE
GRENADIER GUARDS
DIED ON 25TH SEPTEMBER 1916 AGED 26
BURIED IN GUARDS' CEMETERY, LESBOEUFS, FRANCE

Douglas Oliphant's inscription comes from an ode by Ben Jonson (1572-1637), *To the immortal memory and friendship of that noble pair, Sir Lucius Cary & Sir H Morison.* The relevant verse reads:

> It is not growing like a tree
> In bulk, doth make a man better be;
> Or, standing long an oak, three hundred year,
> To fall a log, at last, dry, bald, and sear:
> A lily of a day
> Is fairer far, in May,
> Although it fall, and die that night;
> It was the plant, and flower of light.
> In small proportions, we just beauties see:
> And in short measures, life may perfect be.

From a memorial plaque in his home church at Traquair, we learn that Lieutenant Oliphant was:

> Killed at the Battle of the Somme
> September 25th 1916. Aged 26 years
> Commanding a company and "most
> Gallantly leading his men into action".
> Laid to rest on the battlefield.

Constable, a lieutenant, was 'Commanding a company' because his Company Commander, Captain Spencer-Churchill had been wounded several days earlier. 'Laid to rest on the battlefield', means that Constable was buried where he fell and the grave then lost. It was obviously still lost when this plaque was erected. However, in August 1919 it was discovered at map reference 57c.T.3.c.3.8. and re-buried in the Guards' Cemetery at Lesboeufs.

DICKON
3RD SON OF RICHARD ROSS RUTHERFORD, ROXBURGH, SCOTLAND

SECOND LIEUTENANT RICHARD (DICKON) ROSS, MC
DEVONSHIRE REGIMENT
DIED ON 25TH SEPTEMBER 1916 AGED 22
BURIED IN GUARDS' CEMETERY, LESBOEUFS, FRANCE

Dickon Ross was the third of Richard and Emily Ross's five sons, three of whom were killed in the war. James, the eldest, a Scottish rugby international who played for the London Scottish and the Barbarians, was killed on 1 November 1914; Dickon was killed on 25 September 1916 and eighteen-year-old Thomas, fatally wounded on 4 November 1918 during the Battle of the Sambre, Germany's last-ditch stand on the Sambre-Oise Canal and the last battle of the war, died on the 13th, two days after the Armistice. Their father, Richard Ross, farmed over 1,000 acres around Maxton in Roxburghshire. However, father died in 1908 and Emily Ross moved from Rutherford Farmhouse, Maxton via Starrock Court in Chipstead, Surrey, where she lived during the war, to Sherborne in Dorset. Nevertheless, she thought of Maxton as her sons' home and although James has no grave and is commemorated on the Menin Gate, both Dickon's inscription and that of his brother, Thomas, reference Rutherford, the place where they were born. Second Lieutenant Thomas Ross, Cameron Highlanders, was buried at Premont British Cemetery. His inscription reads:

> Youngest son of Richard Ross
> Rutherford, Maxton, Scotland

You may rest assured That I shall have Done my duty

CAPTAIN JOHN EDWARD NEWDIGATE POYNTZ DENNING
LINCOLNSHIRE REGIMENT
DIED ON 26TH SEPTEMBER 1916 AGED 23
BURIED IN HEILLY STATION CEMETERY, MERICOURT-L'ABBE, FRANCE

This inscription comes from Jack Denning's last letter to his parents:

> Sept 24th '16, 10.30 am
> My own Dearest Mother & Dad,
> This may or may not be my last letter to you, as we are in for it I think tomorrow. I sincerely hope it will be successful. At all events I am determined to go in and win as I know you would have me do. I know you may think this is rather ridiculous especially if I come through alright.
> But you may rest assured that should I get pipped I shall have done my duty, and always remember it is far better to die with honour than to live in shame.
> ... The main object is that to please me, do not worry if I do get pipped. ... Well darlings, best love to all I know. I am
> Ever your loving Boy,
> Jack

What happened the next day is recorded in the 1st Battalion Lincolnshire Regiment War Diary:

> As the hands of the watches touched zero Captain J. Edes and Captain J.E.P.N. Denning, ... followed by their men, sprang over the parapet of Gap Trench ... Both companies had advanced about fifty yards when they came into the enemy's artillery barrage from the right and machine gun fire from the right front. In spite of heavy casualties, there was no wavering until the brigade front line was reached. ...

By this time Captain Denning and all the senior N.C.O.s of C Company had been wounded. Denning died the next day.

HE LOVED DUTY
AND HE FEARED NOT DEATH

CAPTAIN BRYAN DOLPHIN PAULL
ROYAL IRISH RIFLES ATTACHED EAST SURREY REGIMENT
DIED ON 30TH SEPTEMBER 1916 AGED 19
BURIED IN BLIGHTY VALLEY CEMETERY, AUTHUILLE WOOD, FRANCE

Bryan Paull left school, Charterhouse, in the summer of 1914 aged seventeen and enlisted in the army on the outbreak of war. He was gazetted Lieutenant in February 1915, and promoted Captain two months later. He was eighteen and one month, surely one of the youngest Captains of the war. He was nineteen and nine months when he was killed leading an attack on the Schwaben Redoubt on 30 September 1916. The regimental history of the East Surrey Regiment records that 'besides being a most capable officer, [he] was held in great affection by everyone in the Battalion'. Paull's mother chose his inscription; his father was dead. It is not a quotation but it does bear a passing resemblance to a familiar quotation spoken by Brutus in Shakespeare's *Julius Caesar*. However, there is an interesting change of emphasis. Brutus said, I love honour more than I fear death'. For nineteen-year-old Bryan Paull it was 'duty'.

TROS RYDDID A'I WLAD

PRIVATE WILLIAM ROBERTS
ROYAL ARMY MEDICAL CORPS
DIED ON 2ND OCTOBER 1916 AGED 49
BURIED IN BLIGHTY VALLEY CEMETERY, AUTHUILLE WOOD, FRANCE

William Roberts' Welsh inscription translates as 'For freedom and country'. Roberts served as a private in the 56th Field Ambulance, a front line medical unit that usually consisted of ten officers and about 224 men. Privates could be wagon orderlies, stretcher-bearers, cooks or washermen. There is no indication which role Private Roberts fulfilled, but at 49 he was old to be serving in the army.

Field Ambulances were the second point in the casualty evacuation chain; the first point being the Regimental Aid Post situated just a few yards behind the front line. These had no holding capacity and could only administer basic first aid. More serious cases were taken directly to an Advanced Dressing Station, managed by the Field Ambulances. This sometimes necessitated stretcher-bearers carrying the casualty over several miles of ground that was impassable to any form of wheeled transport. When this was the case there were a series of collecting and relay posts along the way. Field Ambulances also had no holding capacity but they were equipped to do more serious emergency work, which later in the war did include surgery. After this, horse or motor ambulances would take the casualty to a Casualty Clearing Station located several miles behind the front line.

The 56th Field Ambulance was part of the 53rd Brigade, 18th Division, which was involved during late September, early October in the continuing struggle for the Schwaben Redoubt. William Roberts was killed on 2 October, the day the Germans launched a big counter-attack, which saw them regain a little of their lost ground.

AGED 17 YEARS
R.I.P.

PRIVATE HUGH AUBREY COCKERTON
CAMBRIDGESHIRE REGIMENT
DIED ON 2ND OCTOBER 1916 AGED 17
BURIED IN DOULLENS COMMUNAL CEMETERY EXTENSION NO. 1

Sep. 10

[To Mrs Sorley]

I am writing on behalf of a gallant youngster in my company, and I believe known to you. His age is I suspect not more than 17 now, and he has been out some while, and though he is an excellent sturdy youngster his nerves are obviously not strong enough for the racket of this existence, which is now-a-days more violent than usual. The point therefore is that his parents or guardian can write and claim him back, by producing a birth certificate, only he himself is apparently entirely in the dark as to who his guardian is – he has of course no parents. So I wonder if you could make representations in the right quarter and collect a copy of his birth certificate and get the thing done: he isn't a fellow I want to lose, but I feel it partakes rather of cruelty to animals to keep him out here just at present.

The letter writer Captain Arthur Innes Adam, Cambridgeshire Regiment, was killed six days later. The 'gallant youngster', Private Hugh Aubrey Cockerton, died of gas poisoning on 2 October before anything could be done to send him home. His father had died in 1907 and although his mother was still alive, she died four months later in February 1917. A Miss Cockerton chose his inscription; perhaps one of his several sisters, making sure that from now on there should be no mistake about his age.

YE BABBLING WINDS
THROUGH SILENCE SWEEP
DISTURB YE NOT
OUR LOVED ONE'S SLEEP

DRIVER THOMAS GRANT HAMILTON
ROYAL FIELD ARTILLERY
DIED ON 3RD OCTOBER 1916 AGED 22
BURIED IN RIBEMONT COMMUNAL CEMETERY EXTENSION, SOMME, FRANCE

This inscription comes from Robert Burns' *Ode for General Washington's Birthday* (1793):

> Where is that soul of Freedom fled?
> Immingled with the mighty dead,
>
> ...
>
> Ye babbling winds! in silence sweep,
> Disturb not ye the hero's sleep,

Hamilton's parents use 'loved one's' rather than 'hero's'; did they know the circumstances of their son's death? Thomas Hamilton was executed on 3 October 1916 for striking a senior officer. The officer, a Second Lieutenant, had put him under open arrest for having a cigarette in his mouth during the mid-day stable parade. The officer then refused to hear Hamilton's explanation at which point Hamilton lost his temper and hit him.

Brought to trial on 20 September Hamilton was found guilty and condemned to death. In ninety per cent of cases death sentences were commuted but the Commander of the 6th Division decided that, 'the state of discipline in this unit requires an example'. General Rawlinson felt that the officer hadn't handled the situation well but Haig disagreed and Hamilton was executed on 3 October.

Did his parents know? Yes. Until November 1917 the next-of-kin of the executed received a letter stating:

> I am directed to inform you that a report has been received from the War Office to the effect that ____ was sentenced after being tried by court martial to suffer death by being shot, and his sentence was duly executed on ____.
>
> *For the Sake of Example*, Anthony Babington, Paladin 1985, p. 83

HE WAS NOT TO KNOW
THE REASON WHY
BUT TO GO AND DIE

PRIVATE WALTER STEPHEN SPRINGETT
LONDON REGIMENT, KENSINGTON BATTALION
DIED ON 5TH OCTOBER 1916 AGED 23
BURIED IN GUARDS' CEMETERY LESBOEUFS, FRANCE

This inscription is Mr and Mrs Springett's own version of the famous lines from the second verse of Tennyson's *The Charge of the Light Brigade*:

> "Forward the Light Brigade!"
> Was there a man dismay'd?
> Not tho' the soldier knew
> Some one had blunder'd:
> Theirs not to make reply,
> Theirs not to reason why,
> Theirs but to do and die:
> Into the valley of Death
> Rode the six hundred.

Tennyson wrote the poem in praise of absolute military loyalty and obedience, even in the face of the certain knowledge that someone high up 'had blunder'd'. Is there admiration or criticism in the Springett's choice of inscription?

Walter Springett was the second of five brothers; his younger brother Frank, serving with the King's Royal Rifle Corps, died of wounds in German captivity on 26 August 1916. His headstone in Grand-Seraucourt British Cemetery reads:

> His name will ever be
> Treasured in our hearts

FELLOWSHIP IS HEAVEN AND THE LACK OF FELLOWSHIP IS HELL

BRIGADIER GENERAL PHILIP HOWELL, CMG
GENERAL STAFF
DIED ON 7TH OCTOBER 1916 AGED 37
BURIED IN VARENNES MILITARY CEMETERY, FRANCE

The stereotypical British First World War general in the public mind is ancient, incompetent, callous and out of touch, and this stereotype still holds good for many people. Brigadier General Philip Howell bore no resemblance to this. To begin with he was only 37 when he died. Professor Gary Sheffield sums him up in *Command and Morale: The British Army on the Western Front 1914-1918*: 'Howell was an intellectual, something of a Bohemian, and a political radical'. His unusual character shows in his letters, for example this to his wife in September 1915:

> It is VILE that all my time should be devoted to killing Germans whom
> I don't in the least want to kill. If all Germany could be united in one
> man and he and I could be shut up together just to talk things out, we
> could settle the war, I feel, in less than one hour. ... Shall I desert and
> see if any of them will listen on the other side?

Far from being out of touch, Howell, frequently visited the front line trenches in order to see the situation for himself. It was whilst on one of these forays that he was killed by a stray shell.

His wife chose his inscription. It sounds like a forthright statement of what life is going to be like now that she has lost her husband's 'fellowship', his companionship. This may have been what she meant but the quotation comes from William Morris's novel about the Peasants' Revolt, *A Dream of John Ball*. Morris holds that fellowship – mutual respect and mutual support – should be the basis of a new society. For Morris it was a political statement, a socialist statement, and knowing that Philip Howell was a political radical, Mrs Howell probably meant it as such too.

> Fellowship is heaven, and the lack of fellowship is hell: fellowship is life,
> and the lack of fellowship is death.

O MEMORIES
THAT BLESS AND BURN
O BARREN GAIN
AND BITTER LOSS

SECOND LIEUTENANT R.F. BATH
LONDON REGIMENT
DIED ON 7TH OCTOBER 1916 AGED 29
BURIED IN GUARDS' CEMETERY, LESBOEUFS, FRANCE

Mrs Ethel Bath was not the only person to choose an inscription from this hugely popular romantic song, *The Rosary*, which is about loss and the acceptance of loss. Written in America in 1898 by Ethelbert Nevin and Robert Cameron Rogers, it became one of the most popular songs of the early twentieth century, made even more popular by Florence L Barclay's novel of the same name in which the song plays a central part. Barclay's book was published in 1909 and immediately became a bestseller on both sides of the Atlantic; by 1924 it had sold a million copies.

> The hours I spent with thee, dear heart,
> Are as a string of pearls to me.
> I count them over every one apart,
> My rosary.
> Each hour a pearl, each pearl a prayer,
> To still a heart in absence wrung.
> I tell each bead unto the end — and there
> A cross is hung.
> Oh memories that bless — and burn!
> Oh, barren gain — and bitter loss!
> I kiss each bead, and strive at last to learn
> To kiss the cross,
> Sweetheart,
> To kiss the cross.

Ethel Bath never remarried and died in on 12 September 1967. There do not appear to have been any children from the marriage.

GUARDS'
CEMETERY,
LESBOEUFS

"THIS HAPPY-STARRED FULL-BLOODED SPIRIT SHOOTS INTO THE SPIRITUAL LAND" R.L.S.

PRIVATE FRANK WILLIAM TROTMAN
LONDON REGIMENT, PRINCE OF WALES' OWN CIVIL SERVICE RIFLES
DIED ON 7TH OCTOBER 1916 AGED 33
BURIED IN WARLENCOURT BRITISH CEMETERY, FRANCE

This is a strong and unusual inscription. It comes from *Aes Triplex*, an essay by Robert Louis Stevenson in which, knowing that he himself doesn't have long to live, he urges people to rush headlong into life even if death is just round the corner: better to be taken at the flood than at low tide. Aes triplex is Latin for triple bronze; battle armour was made of triple bronze and thought to be indestructible. To Stevenson, the spirit of someone who dies in the fullness of life is similarly indestructible. The following long but edited passage gives an indication of his meaning:

> It is better to lose life like a spendthrift than to waste it like a miser. It is better to live and be done with it, than die daily in the sick room. ... does not life go down with a better grace, foaming in full body over a precipice, than miserably straggling to an end in sandy deltas? When the Greeks made their fine saying that those whom the Gods love die young, I cannot help believing they had this sort of death also in their eye. ... In the hot-fit of life, a-tiptoe on the highest point of being, he passes at a bound on to the other side. ... the trumpets are hardly done blowing, when, trailing with him clouds of glory, this happy-starred, full-blooded spirit shoots into the spiritual land.

Mr WG Trotman of 88 Lower Kennington Lane, London SE11 signed the form confirming Frank Trotman's inscription. This was probably his father, George Trotman of Trotman & Co, tea dealers and grocers operating from that address. Frank was educated at St Olave's Grammar School, worked for London County Council and was killed in action in the 47th (2nd London) Division attack on Transloy Ridge.

NOTHING BUT WELL AND FAIR
AND WHAT MAY QUIET US
IN A DEATH SO NOBLE

SERJEANT LESLIE COULSON
LONDON REGIMENT, ROYAL FUSILIERS
DIED ON 8TH OCTOBER 1916 AGED 27
BURIED IN GROVE TOWN CEMETERY, MEAULTE, FRANCE

Leslie Coulson was a journalist, the assistant foreign editor of the *London Standard*, and a pastoral poet. There is a pastoral strain evident in his war poetry too; it still referred to lanes and larks and cornflowers but now in conjunction with thundering guns, screaming shells and dead bodies. Coulson enlisted in September 1914; in the autumn of 1916 he was on the Somme. On 7 October, during an attack on Dewdrop Trench, Coulson was shot in the chest by a sniper and died the next day. Frederick Coulson, Leslie's father, chose from the opening lines of Milton's *Samson Agonistes* for his son's inscription:

> Nothing is here for tears, nothing to wail
> Or knock the breast, no weakness, no contempt,
> Dispraise, or blame, nothing but well and fair,
> And what may quiet us in a death so noble.

Nothing for tears ... only the fact that Coulson would never 'come home':

> When I come home, and leave behind
> Dark things, I would not call to mind,
> I'll taste good ale and home-made bread,
> And see white sheets and pillows spread.
> And there is one who'll softly creep
> To kiss me ere I fall asleep,
> And tuck me 'neath the counterpane,
> And I shall be a boy again
> When I come home!

> *When I Come Home*
> Leslie Coulson

THE YOUNGEST OF THREE BROTHERS WHO GAVE THEIR LIVES FOR HUMANITY

LANCE CORPORAL OSWALD RAYMOND GOODYEAR
NEWFOUNDLAND REGIMENT
DIED ON 12TH OCTOBER 1916 AGED 18
BURIED IN BANCOURT BRITISH CEMETERY, FRANCE

A combination of the Newfoundland Regiment's digitised records and an acclaimed family memoir, *The Danger Tree*, written by David Macfarlane, one of the surviving brother's grandsons, means that a great deal is known about Oswald and his five brothers, two of whom were also killed in the war. One of the brothers, Hedley, who served with the Canadian Infantry, wrote a letter to his mother on 7 August 1918, the eve of the opening of the battle of Amiens, which became famous as the last letter of Hedley Goodyear. It was read at Armistice and Memorial Day services for many years:

> This is the evening of the attack and my thoughts are with you all at home.
> ... With hope for mankind and with visions of a new world a blow will be
> struck tomorrow which will definitely mark the turn of the tide. It will be
> one of a grand series of victories which will humble the selfish and barbarous
> foeman and will exalt the hearts that are suffering for freedom. In a few
> moments I shall make the final address to my men and shall strengthen their
> hearts, if they need strengthening, with the language of men of war! We shall
> strive only to achieve victory. We shall not hold our lives dear.

In fact, his last letter was the one he wrote ten days later on 17 August in which he told his mother that he was 'hun-proof'. He was shot and killed by a German sniper five days later. He is buried in Hillside Cemetery on the Somme where his inscription reads:

> Beneath this stone
> A hero sleeps
> Who gave his life
> For humanity.

LONSDALE CEMETERY,
AUTHUILLE

KILLED AT
THE SCHWABEN REDOUBT
SUAVITER IN MODO
FORTITER IN RE

LIEUTENANT ALFRED ROYAL BRADFORD
CAMBRIDGESHIRE REGIMENT
DIED ON 14ᵀᴴ OCTOBER 1916 AGED 22
BURIED IN LONSDALE CEMETERY, AUTHUILLE, FRANCE

On 14 October 1916 the 1ˢᵗ Battalion the Cambridgeshire Regiment, together with the 4/5ᵗʰ Black Watch, succeeded in not only capturing but also in holding the Schwaben Redoubt, an event described by General Haig as 'one of the finest feats of arms in the history of the British Army'. Constructed of trenches, dugouts and machine gun emplacements, the redoubt was an 'all-important hill-top, which dominated the field of battle for many miles in every direction'. Six attempts had been made to capture it since 1 July, and many hundreds of men had been killed in these attempts. Cambridgeshire took great pride in their regiment's success, which explains why Marcus Bradford, manager and later owner of the University Arms Hotel in Cambridge, mentioned it on his son's headstone inscription.

There is no record of how Bradford was killed but his commanding officer, Lt Colonel Clayton, co-author of *The Cambridgeshires 1914-1919*, writes how at the end of the day:

> I went out into the still, starlit night. By the entrance to my dug-out lay the body of my brave intelligence officer, Bradford. Fearless in life, he had done his work nobly. I am afraid I sobbed like a child; but I was not ashamed of this breakdown.

The Latin quotation, forming the second part of the inscription, casts a little more light on Bradford's character: 'Suaviter in modo, fortiter in re', gentle in manner, resolute in deed. The quotation comes from *Industria ad Curandos Animae Morbos* written by the Jesuit priest Claudio Acquviva (1543-1615).

M.A. HONS. GLASG.
B.A. HONS. OXON.

SECOND LIEUTENANT GRAHAM BRYMNER THOMAS JARDINE
ARGYLL AND SUTHERLAND HIGHLANDERS
DIED ON 18TH OCTOBER 1916 AGED 24
BURIED IN WARLENCOURT BRITISH CEMETERY, FRANCE

Graham Jardine was a scholar – as his parents were proud to imply on his headstone inscription. He was, in fact, the top scholar of Glasgow Academy in 1908, the holder of two prizes at Glasgow University and of a Lodge Exhibition at University College, Oxford. In July 1915 Jardine took a commission in the Argyll and Sutherland Highlanders and in May 1916, attached to the 5th Battalion the Cameron Highlanders, went to France. He was killed five months later in an attack on the Butte de Warlencourt. These are the bare bones of his life. However, in the Marquis de Ruvigny's *Roll of Honour*, a friend has provided us with a brief personal insight:

> I never met a man who had less fear of death. We talked of it more than once … He always said that to give one's life for a cause one believed in was the most intense kind of self-realization that anyone could achieve.

AMOR PATRIAE

PRIVATE THOMAS JAMES REYNARD
SOUTH AFRICAN INFANTRY
DIED ON 18TH OCTOBER 1916 AGED 29
BURIED IN WARLENCOURT BRITISH CEMETERY, FRANCE

'Amor patriae', love of the fatherland. has greater associations than this straight translation indicates. It's a quote from Virgil's *Aeneid*: 823: 'Vincit amor patriae laudumque immensa cupido', where it attempts to explain the difficult decision Brutus took for 'amor patriae'. And the difficult decision – he had his two sons executed for treason. Brutus is always seen as the great Roman example of the man who loved his country above all else, even above his sons, but Virgil, by this comment, implies that behind this was also an excessive lust for praise, 'immensa cupido'.

In the Reynard family, who was it that loved their fatherland, the land of their birth? Thomas James Reynard, and his brother Fred Henry, were born in Britain but had lived in South Africa since they were infants. They both served in A Company 1st Regiment South African Infantry, and were both killed on 18 October 1916 in an attack on the Butte de Warlencourt. Love of the mother country, Britain, was strong throughout the Empire, even among the young so it would not have been unusual for Thomas and Fred to have wanted to fight for her. But, love of the mother country must have been strong in their parents too and it was their father, Charles Reynard, who confirmed the inscription. Did he in any way associate himself with Brutus? There was no conscription in South Africa. Did he blame himself for encouraging his sons to fight in the war that killed them? John Buchan, in his *History of the South African Forces in France*, describes how at 3.40 am on the morning of 18 October, the South Africans attacked in the most atrocious conditions, it was raining heavily and the ground was a quagmire. Sixty-nine of the one hundred men of C Company became casualties, but of A and B companies there was virtually no trace. The Kings Own Scottish Borderers later took the ground and in his memoir, *Three Years With the 9th Division*, Lt Colonel WD Croft wrote of coming across, 'a large party of South Africans at full stretch with bayonets at the charge – all dead'. Only Thomas Reynard has a grave and an inscription, Fred Reynard is commemorated on the Thiepval Memorial.

AQUILA NON CAPTAT MUSCAS

LIEUTENANT D'ARCY REIN WADSWORTH
CANADIAN INFANTRY
DIED ON 18TH OCTOBER 1916 AGED 23
BURIED IN CONTAY BRITISH CEMETERY, FRANCE

Aquila non captat muscas – the eagle does not catch flies – what kind of an epitaph is this? It's a Latin proverb, an admonishment to spend your time on worthwhile endeavours not to waste it on trivia, not to get distracted but to concentrate on your goal, just as an eagle only pursues quality prey not flies. Employed at the Bank of Montreal, D'Arcy Rein Wadsworth enlisted in May 1915 and was commissioned into the Canadian Infantry the following month. Sent to England in June 1916 with the 75th Battalion, he was in Flanders by August and on the Somme in September. Sometime during these months Wadsworth attended a bombing course and was subsequently appointed battalion bombing officer. On 14 October the Battalion came out of the trenches at Tara Hill and two days later Wadsworth was mortally wounded taking a bombing practice when one of the bombs exploded prematurely. He died two days later.

YR YDYM NI YNER GARU EF AM IDDO EF YN GYNTAF EIN CARU NI

PRIVATE THOMAS ROSSER DAVIES
1ST CANADIAN MOUNTED RIFLES
DIED ON 19TH OCTOBER 1916 AGED 25
BURIED IN CONTAY BRITISH CEMETERY, FRANCE

A Welsh wife chose this Welsh inscription for her Welsh husband who was killed on 19 October 1916 whilst serving with the 1st Canadian Mounted Rifles. The family came from Ammanford, Carmarthenshire, Wales. Davies was born in Ammanford and his wife's address after his death was in Ammanford. There is no evidence that Davies was ever in Canada. Might he just have been drafted into the Canadian Mounted Rifles to replace their casualties rather than having been a Canadian?

Davies' inscription quotes the First Epistle of John Chapter 4 verse 19, 'We love him because he first loved us'. Did his wife, Mrs Annie Davies, notice the next verse: 'If a man say, I love God, and hateth his brother, he is a liar: for he that loveth not his brother whom he hath seen, how can he love God whom he hath not seen?' Or was she purposely making a veiled criticism about war?

There is no information about how Davies met his death but the 1st Canadian Mounted Rifles were not in the trenches on the day he died, and as he's buried at Contay British Cemetery where two Canadian Casualty Clearing Stations were based, he is most likely to have died of wounds received between the 9th and the 13th October when the Battalion were last in the front line. For these four days the battalion war diary recorded that 13, 2, 37 and 17 other ranks were wounded on each of the successive days, days when it usually described things as 'situation normal with intermittent shelling', and occasionally, 'hostile enemy activity'.

HE GAVE HIS ALL FOR FREEDOM
THE WHOLE WIDE WORLD TO SAVE

PRIVATE ADON SMITH
CANADIAN INFANTRY
DIED BETWEEN 21ST AND 22ND OCTOBER 1916 AGED 26
BURIED IN ADANAC MILITARY CEMETERY, MIRAUMONT, FRANCE

Adon Smith was an American citizen, the son of Adon and Emilie T Smith of 233 West 48th Street, New York. According to the 87th Battalion Canadian Expeditionary Force Nominal Roll, Adon Smith had previously served in the US Army. He was taken on the Canadian strength on 21 January 1916 and was killed in action sometime between the 21st and the 22nd October 1916 during the Canadian assault on Regina Ridge. The Battalion war diary, in recording what happened, throws light on the reason for the imprecision of Smith's date of death:

> 'D' Company reinforced the Battalion during the night of Oct. 21-22. During the attack and the following two days there were 281 casualties, of all ranks, including all but one of the officers who participated in the attack.

Adon Smith's mother confirmed his inscription, passionately stating the cause for which she believed her son had given his life.

Amicus usque ad aras
Gus am bris an la
Agud an teich
Na sgaillean

SERJEANT ALASDAIR MARTIN
SEAFORTH HIGHLANDERS
DIED ON 23RD OCTOBER 1916 AGED 22
BURIED IN GUARDS' CEMETERY LESBOEUFS, FRANCE

Serjeant Martin's inscription combines a Latin saying with a Scottish Gaelic quote from the Old Testament. The Latin – amicus usque ad aras – translates as 'a friend to the altars', with the meaning a friend until death. This is no doubt the meaning Alasdair Martin's mother intended. However, according to Plutarch, when Pericles described his friendship in this way he was putting a limit on it. Roman oaths were taken at altars, it was like swearing on the Holy Bible, and Pericles was telling his friend that his friendship with him would go as far as the altars but no further, he would never swear an oath on the altar for him. The second part of the inscription, 'Gus am bris an la agud an teich na sgaillean' is a quotation from the Song of Solomon 4:6, 'Until the day break, and the shadows flee away'. It's a popular inscription in all languages but, like the Latin inscription above, it now has another meaning from the one originally intended. For Mrs Martin, when the day breaks and the shadows flee away is a reference to the time when the living will be reunited with their dead at their own deaths. In the Song of Solomon the words are spoken by a lover relishing the fact that he can be with his beloved all night ... until the day breaks. Six soldiers died on 23 October 1916 and were buried at map reference 57c.T.9.b.2.8. In August 1919 the Graves Registration Unit exhumed their bodies and was able to identify five of them as being members of the 2nd Battalion Seaforth Highlanders, including Sergeant Martin. All were re-buried in the Guards' Cemetery, Lesboeufs.

Eternall Gratitude
For the Short Enjoyment
Of so Sweet a Mercie

SECOND LIEUTENANT STEPHEN KNOWLES
RIFLE BRIGADE
DIED ON 24TH OCTOBER 1916 AGED 20
BURIED IN GROVE TOWN CEMETERY, MEAULTE, FRANCE

This tender inscription has an obscure origin. It comes from a memorial in the church of St Mary the Virgin, Gilston, Hertfordshire, dedicated to Bridget, the four-year-old daughter of Sir John and Lady Gore, who died in 1657:

> ... who Being the most desired Fruit of many prayers, and the joy of her Mother's heart, was without reluctancie, most chearfullie resigned to God that gave her in the 4th yeare, the blossome of her age, the 10th of February 1657. In testimony whereof & of her dearest affection to her most ravishing memorie, shee hath erected this small monument & deposited in the hands of the Officers of this Parish 60L. to be disposed in land, and the revenue of it for a perpetuall pious and charitable Anniversary of her eternall gratitude for the short enjoyment of so sweet a mercie.

Stephen Knowles was born and brought up in Bolton in Lancashire where both his parents were also born and where his father was a master cotton spinner. How was his mother, who chose the inscription, his father having died in 1912, familiar with a monument in a Hertfordshire church? The inscription was printed in *The Historical Antiquities of Hertfordshire*, 1826, and again in *The Christian Remembrancer*, 1841, but Mrs Knowles spelt it as it was on the monument and neither of these publications did. Educated at Repton School and destined for Pembroke College, Cambridge to read medicine, Stephen Knowles joined up on the outbreak of war and was gazetted a second lieutenant in the Rifle Brigade on 15 May 1915. He went to France on 6 December and died on 24 October 1916 of wounds received in an attack on the German trenches at Guadecourt the previous day.

In loving memory
"These are they" –

LIEUTENANT GEORGE GORDON STEVEN
MACHINE GUN SECTION (HEAVY BRANCH)
DIED ON 24TH OCTOBER 1916 AGED 23
BURIED IN BLIGHTY VALLEY CEMETERY, AUTHUILLE WOOD, FRANCE

Who are the 'they' referred to in this inscription? The answer is in the Book of Revelation 7:14, 'These are they which came out of great tribulation, and they have washed their robes, and made them white in the blood of the lamb'. The words will have been more familiar to people from the second verse of Isaac Watts' hymn, *How Bright These Glorious Visions Shine:*

> Lo! these are they from sufferings great
> Who came to realms of light;
> And in the blood of Christ have washed
> Those robes that shine so bright.

The consolation of death to those who mourn is that the dead are now 'safe'; nothing can hurt them. For Shelley's *Adonais*, 'envy and calumny and hate and pain ... can touch him not again', whereas for Binyon's young soldiers, 'age shall not weary them nor the years condemn'. Watts' dead are similarly safe:

> Hunger and thirst are felt no more
> Nor suns with scorching ray;
> God is their Sun, whose cheering beams
> Diffuse eternal day.

And not only are the dead safe but those who mourn will be comforted, 'And God the Lord from every eye shall wipe off every tear'.

George Gordon Steven, a graduate of Glasgow Academy and Technical College, was a marine engineer. He served originally with the Loyal North Lancashire Regiment before transferring first to the Machine Gun Corps, and then to the Heavy Section, which provided the first tanks crews.

LIEUTENANT
GEORGE GORDON STEVEN
HEAVY SECTION, M.G.C.
(LATER TANK CORPS)
24TH OCTOBER 1916

IN LOVING MEMORY
"THESE ARE THEY"

LIEUTENANT STEVEN'S
HEADSTONE IN BLIGHTY
VALLEY, CEMETERY,
AUTHUILLE WOOD

LIFE IS ETERNAL
AND LOVE IS IMMORTAL
AND DEATH IS ONLY A HORIZON

LIEUTENANT GUY JOHN HAMILTON ASHWIN
DURHAM LIGHT INFANTRY
DIED ON 11TH NOVEMBER 1916 AGED 22
BURIED IN WARLENCOURT BRITISH CEMETERY, FRANCE

Lieutenant Ashwin was killed in the Durham Light Infantry's attempt to capture the Butte de Warlencourt, which they succeeded temporarily in doing only to be driven off again with huge casualties. The Butte, thought to be a prehistoric burial mound, is several hundred feet high and gives its possessors a strategic advantage over the surrounding flat countryside. The British did not succeed in capturing it until February 1917. Guy Ashwin's inscription is a line from a prayer written by William Penn (1644-1718), the Quaker founder of Pennsylvania. Later modified by Rossiter W Raymond (1840-1918), it is to him that the Internet usually attributes the authorship.

> We seem to give them back to Thee, O God, who gavest them to us. Yet, as thou didst not lose them in giving, so do we not lose them by their return. Not as the world giveth, givest Thou, O Lover of Souls. What Thou givest, Thou takest not away. For what is Thine is ours also if we are Thine. And life is eternal and love is immortal, and death is only an horizon, and an horizon is nothing save the limit of our sight. Lift us up, strong Son of God, that we may see further; cleanse our eyes that we may know ourselves to be nearer to our loved ones who art with Thee. And while Thou dost prepare a place for us, prepare us also for that happy place, that where Thou art we may be also for evermore.

In proud memory
Shall we not also
Take the ebb
That had the flow

SECOND LIEUTENANT FRANK SIDNEY CHESTERTON
ROYAL FIELD ARTILLERY
DIED ON 11TH NOVEMBER 1916 AGED 39
BURIED IN GROVE TOWN CEMETERY, MEAULTE, FRANCE

Frank Chesterton's wife, Norah, chose this inscription from a poem by W.E. Henley called *What is to Come*, a tender, bittersweet poem, very appropriate for a wife's farewell:

> What is to come we know not. But we know
> That what has been was good – was good to show,
> Better to hide, and best of all to bear.
> We are the masters of the days that were;
> We have lived, we have loved, we have suffered ... even so.
>
> Shall we not take the ebb who had the flow?
> Life was our friend? Now, if it be our foe –
> Dear, though it spoil and break us! – need we care
> What is to come?
>
> Let the great winds their worst and wildest blow,
> Or the gold weather round us mellow slow;
> We have fulfilled ourselves, and we can dare
> And we can conquer, though we may not share
> In the rich quiet of the afterglow
> What is to come.

Frank Chesterton was a successful architect working mainly in London and the Home Counties, particularly in Knightsbridge and Kensington where much of the rebuilding of the High Street during the early years of the twentieth century came from his designs. He was also a partner in the family's residential property business, Chesterton and Sons, which his grandfather had started and which his son, Oliver, successfully expanded into one of London's largest estate agencies.

HE VOLUNTEERED
HE THOUGHT IT WAS HIS DUTY
HE DIED THAT WE MIGHT LIVE

PRIVATE JOHN THOMAS JARDINE
CANADIAN INFANTRY
DIED ON 11TH NOVEMBER 1916 AGED 20
BURIED IN VILLERS STATION CEMETERY, VILLERS-AU-BOIS, FRANCE

'He thought it was his duty', there is a sense that we have been given an insight into Private Jardine's thought processes. Did the Mrs Robina D Duncan of Waskada, Manitoba, Canada who chose the inscription know him? If so it has not been possible to discover who she was. The final line of the inscription, 'he died that we might live', comes from the poem *Hail! – and Farewell!* published in a collection of verse by John Oxenham entitled '*All's Well' Some Helpful Verse for These Dark Days of* War, 1915. John Oxenham was the pseudonym of the novelist, poet and hymn writer William Arthur Dunkerley.

They died that we might live, –
Hail! – And Farewell!
– All honour give
To those who, nobly striving, nobly fell,
That we might live!

That we might live they died, –
Hail! – And Farewell!
– Their courage tried,
By every mean device of treacherous hate,
Like Kings they died.

Eternal honour give, –
Hail! – And Farewell!
– To those who died,
In that full splendour of heroic pride,
That we might live!

WE'LL MEET AGAIN
WHEN THE BARRAGE LIFTS

ABLE SEAMAN JOHN CARRUTHERS FARQUHARSON
ROYAL NAVAL DIVISION VOLUNTEER RESERVE
DIED ON 13TH NOVEMBER 1916 AGED 19
BURIED IN ANCRE BRITISH CEMETERY, BEAUMONT-HAMEL, FRANCE

The object of the artillery barrage is to prevent the enemy from manning his parapets and installing his machine guns in time to arrest the advance of our infantry. ... The barrage must, therefore, be sufficiently heavy to keep the enemy in his dug-outs and shelters as long as possible, and sufficiently accurate to allow the infantry to get so close to the trench attacked that, <u>when the barrage lifts</u>, they can cover the remaining distance before the enemy can prepare to receive them.
Artillery in Offensive Operations April 1916

'When the barrage lifts' is the moment for the infantry to rush the enemy trenches. For many years an *In Memoriam* notice to the 9th and 10th Battalions the King's Own Yorkshire Light Infantry used to appear in *The Times* on 1 July. It would conclude with these words, the toast the adjutant had used on 30 June, the eve of the Somme Offensive.

In the context of the inscription, when the barrage lifts the battle of life will be over allowing James and Jessie Farquharson to be reunited with their nineteen-year-old son and his twenty-one-year-old brother Robert who was killed in action serving with the Royal Engineers on 20 September 1917. Able Seaman John Farquharson served with the Nelson Battalion, Royal Naval Division, which was used as an infantry division throughout the war, first in Gallipoli and then in France. He was killed in action on 13 November 1916 in the assault on Beaumont-Hamel.

I WILL GO FORTH
WHEN I FALL IT MATTERS NOT
SO AS GOD'S WORK IS DONE

LIEUTENANT HERBERT WILLIAM HITCHCOCK
MACHINE GUN CORPS (HEAVY BRANCH)
DIED ON 13TH NOVEMBER 1916 AGED 22
BURIED IN MILL ROAD CEMETERY, THIEPVAL, FRANCE

The Imperial War Museum has a close-up photograph of a ditched Mark I tank showing A13 HMLS 'We're all in it' stencilled on its side. The caption says that this Mark I tank first went into action at the Battle of Messines in June 1917, but in fact 'We're all in it' first went into action on 13 November 1916, and was put out of action that same day, the day Lieutenant Herbert Hitchcock, the officer in charge, was killed. In 1914 Herbert William Hitchcock was studying Classics at Balliol College, Oxford, where he was described as a 'hard-working, rather silent student, with a quiet determination and a great capacity for thinking things out'. In March 1915 he took a commission in the 10th Norfolk Regiment before transferring to the Machine Gun Corps and then to the Heavy Section.

Hitchcock's parents chose his inscription. It comes from a once celebrated poem, *A Life Drama*, from a now little-known Scottish poet, Alexander Smith (1829-1867). This is the relevant passage:

> I will go forth 'mong men, not mailed in scorn,
> But in the armour of pure intent.
> Great duties are before me and great songs,
> And whether crowned or crownless when I fall,
> It matters not, so as God's work is done.
> I've learned to prize the quiet lightning-deed,
> Not the applauding thunder at its heels
> Which men call Fame. Our night is past;
> We stand in precious sunrise, and beyond
> A long day stretches to the very end.

MILL ROAD CEMETERY,
THIEPVAL

GOD IS OUR REFUGE
AND STRENGTH
A VERY PRESENT HELP
IN TROUBLE

PRIVATE DONALD MCCALLUM
BLACK WATCH
DIED ON 13TH NOVEMBER 1916 AGED 19
BURIED IN HUNTER'S CEMETERY, BEAUMONT-HAMEL, FRANCE

God is our refuge and strength, a very present help in trouble.

Therefore we will not fear, though the earth be removed, and though the mountains be carried into the midst of the sea;

Though the waters thereof roar and be troubled, though the mountains shake with the swelling thereof.

Psalm 46: 1-3

Donald McCallum was a forester on the Dundas estate in Dunira, Perthshire. His parents, James and Emma McCallum, have used their son's headstone inscription to assert their unshakeable faith in God. McCallum joined up in February 1915 at the age of seventeen. He was sent to France in August 1916 and killed in action three months later in the capture of Beaumont-Hamel.

Beaumont-Hamel had been one of the objectives of the 1 July but had proved to be so heavily fortified that it was virtually impregnable. Eventually, on 13 November, the 51st Division and the 63rd Royal Naval Division, launched a much postponed attack across ground made almost impossible by three weeks of heavy rain. However, with the benefit of surprise and the help of thick fog, by the end of the day they had finally achieved the objective. McCallum and thirty-two other members of the 6th Battalion the Black Watch, all killed on 13 November, are buried in Hunter's Cemetery. This tiny cemetery, which only has forty-one burials, is called Hunter's after one of the two Chaplains to the 6th Battalion who spent 'the days following the fight, searching the battlefield under continuous shell fire, and so well did they carry out this work that every missing man of the Battalion was accounted for'.

History of the Black Watch in the Great War Vol. 2 p.152

HUNTER'S CEMETERY,
BEAUMONT-HAMEL

MY COUNTRY RIGHT OR WRONG

LANCE CORPORAL ARCHIE FERGUSON
ARGYLL AND SUTHERLAND HIGHLANDERS
DIED ON 13TH NOVEMBER 1916 AGED 19
BURIED IN MAILLY WOOD CEMETERY, MAILLY-MAILLET, FRANCE

This phrase represents the ultimate in extreme patriotism, unquestioning allegiance to country, and this is probably the intended meaning of the inscription. However, the phrase has an interesting provenance. In his 1790 pamphlet, *Reflections on the Revolution in France*, the political theorist and philosopher Edmund Burke (1729-1797) wrote, 'To make us love our country, our country ought to be lovely'. In other words, our country should deserve our love not just expect it. In 1816 an American naval officer, Stephen Decatur, raised a toast, 'Our country! in her intercourse with foreign nations, may she always be in the right; but our country, right or wrong'. By the end of the nineteenth century, the phrase had gained a bad reputation with American anti-imperialists. But Senator Carl Schurtz (1829-1906), to whom it is usually attributed, made it very clear what the phrase meant to him in a speech he gave in 1872:

> The Senator from Wisconsin cannot frighten me by exclaiming, 'My country, right or wrong'. In one sense I say too, my country; and my country is the great American Republic. My country, right or wrong; if right to be kept right; and if wrong, to be set right.

For Schurtz, like Burke, a country must deserve its peoples' allegiance.

Archie Ferguson was a clerk in the Greenock branch of the *Glasgow Herald*. He served with the 8th Battalion the Argyll and Sutherland Highlanders, part of the 51st Highland Division, and was killed in action at Beaumont-Hamel.

A SOLDIER OF RABAUL GALLIPOLI & FRANCE HIS DUTY DONE

PRIVATE JAMES FREDERICK BUCKLAND
AUSTRALIAN INFANTRY
DIED ON 14ᵀᴴ NOVEMBER 1916 AGED 22
BURIED IN WARLENCOURT BRITISH CEMETERY, FRANCE

Private Buckland's inscription is a reminder of a forgotten episode from the earliest days of the war. In September 1914, at Britain's request, the Australian Naval and Military Expeditionary Force invaded the island of New Britain, part of German New Guinea. Their orders were to take out a strategically important wireless station at Rabaul, which would otherwise have been of great value to the German East Asiatic Squadron. The successful struggle, known as the Battle of Bita Paka, was Australia's first military engagement of the war. According to his inscription, Private Buckland was part of this Force. As a member of the 19ᵗʰ Battalion Australian Infantry, many of whose members had also been part of this Force, Buckland served in Gallipoli from August to December 1915 and then in France until his death in November 1916 during the Battle of Flers, which was fought in truly terrible conditions of both weather and terrain.

Private Buckland went missing on 14 November. An Australian Red Cross file records his family's attempt to find out what had happened to him – and the difficulties of doing so:

> He is in hospital in England. I am certain of this. Men in the Bn. have heard from him.
> Private Cox 26.2.17

> Private Griggs ... told me in Nov. last that he had seen Buckland killed. He was blown up in a trench at Flers.
> Private Williamson 8.6.17

> I saw Buckland at Weymouth about six weeks ago, in the Westham camp. He had an arm off ...
> Cooper E. 10.9.17

BIRTHLESS DEATHLESS AND CHANGELESS REMAINETH THE SPIRIT FOR EVER

PRIVATE ERNEST GEORGE DORNBUSCH
AUSTRALIAN MACHINE GUN CORPS
DIED ON 14TH NOVEMBER 1916 AGED 27
BURIED IN WARLENCOURT BRITISH CEMETERY, FRANCE

This is an unusual inscription from an unusual source, the *Bhagavad-Gita* a Hindu scripture in which Krishna argues:

> Never the spirit was born; the spirit shall cease to be never; never was time it was not; end and beginning are dreams! Birthless and deathless and changeless remaineth the spirit for ever; death hath not touched it at all, dead though the house of it seems!

There are only three men with the surname Dornbusch who were killed during the First World War and buried in a British war cemetery and the other two are German soldiers: Kanonier Hermann Dornbusch and Obermatrose Karl Johann Dornbusch. Is this why the Australian National War Memorial records his name as Ernest George Dornbush, spelt without the telltale 'c'? This is the way Ernest spelt his name when he enlisted, and the way his mother spelt her name when she signed the form for the Roll of Honour of Australia, although someone has written on the outside of this form, 'correct name Dornbusch', the spelling the War Graves Commission have used. George Ernest Dornbusch was born in London. His parents emigrated to Australia when he was five months old and settled in Sydney, where he attended Sydney Grammar School. An engineer and 'sheep shearing machinery expert', Dornbusch enlisted in April 1915, served in Gallipoli and France and was killed on 14 November 1916. A Red Cross search found a witness who reported:

> I was in company with this man in an attack near Fleurs. I was injured by the shell that killed Durnbush. ... I knew him well, we were in the same gun coy. ... This man was killed instantly but I can give you no details re his burial. I saw him lying dead before I was myself removed to the clearing hospital.
> C. Mallard Dartford Hospital 8.3.17

BROTHER TO A.H. HODGES 13TH BTN. KILLED AT GALLIPOLI

PRIVATE CHARLES FREDERICK HODGES
AUSTRALIAN INFANTRY
DIED ON 14TH NOVEMBER 1916 AGED 23
BURIED IN WARLENCOURT BRITISH CEMETERY, FRANCE

It was nine months before Charles Hodges' parents discovered his fate; nine months in which the Australian Red Cross Wounded and Missing Enquiry Bureau tried to find witnesses who had seen what had happened. Eventually they tracked down Corporal L O'Neill who told them definitively:

> On 14th November at 5 am we were attacking; we failed in our objective and retired to our front line which we held. I saw Hodges after we had got back to our lines about 9 am go outside our trench; there were wounded men inside the trench and he had to go outside to get passed them. A sniper hit him in the head and he died about two minutes after. I was right alongside of him.

Mr and Mrs Hodges did discover what had happened to this son, but they never found out about his elder brother, Albert Henry, who went missing in Gallipoli on 22 August 1915 in the unsuccessful Australian assault on Hill 60. His body was never found and curiously there is no record of his parents instituting a Red Cross search for him. Albert Hodges' name is commemorated on the Lone Pine memorial in Gallipoli and on his brother's grave in France.

FOR HOME AND GLORY
INSERTED BY HIS MOTHER
HELEN MCLAUGHLAN
R.I.P.

PRIVATE PETER MCLAUGHLAN
CAMERONIANS (SCOTTISH RIFLES)
DIED ON 18TH NOVEMBER 1916 AGED 19
BURIED IN LA NEUVILLE COMMUNAL CEMETERY, CORBIE, FRANCE

This doesn't say hope and glory as in 'Land of', but home and glory, the words coming from the last verse of a music hall song, *In the Pale Moonlight*, sung by Vesta Tilley, the male impersonator, whose fame reached its peak during the First World War.

> In the pale moonlight, 'twas an awful sight,
> Upon a field of battle
> Lay boys in red who'd fought and bled,
> Amidst the din and rattle.
> Now the fight was done the victory won,
> And on that field so gory,
> Were the boys who fought as Britons ought,
> For country, home and glory.
> It's British courage, it's deeds like these
> Makes England the mistress of land and seas.

It's obvious from the reference to 'boys in red' that the song predates the First World War since the British Army stopped wearing red jackets when khaki was introduced in 1902. However, for Helen McLaughlan, pride in 'British courage and its deeds', despite the numbers who 'fought and bled', which included her son, seemed to have survived the bloodshed of Flanders. Peter McLaughlan was the youngest of Helen Maclaughlan's four sons. He served with the 5th/6th Battalion The Cameronians, Scottish Rifles, and was killed on the Somme on the last day of the campaign.

The Thiepval
Memorial

Here are recorded
Names of officers
And men of the
British Armies who fell
On the Somme battlefields
July 1915 February 1918
But to whom
The fortune of war
Denied the known
And honoured burial
Given to their
Comrades in death

Epitaphs featured in this book by CWGC Cemetery

Achiet-le-Grand Communal Cemetery Extension
Captain A I Adam   IV.Q.12   page 78

Adanac Military Cemetery, Miraumont
Private A Smith   II.G.11   page 109

Albert Communal Cemetery Extension
Private D Best   I.H.26   page 23
Sapper A Myllymaki   I.K.3   page 63

Ancre British Cemetery, Beaumont-Hamel
Able Seaman JC Farquharson   III.E.6   page 117

Bancourt British Cemetery
Lance Corporal OR Goodyear   VIII.M.5   page 102

Beauval Communal Cemetery
Second Lieutenant WHA Damiano   A9   page 22

Becourt Military Cemetery, Becordel-Becourt
Second Lieutenant RAF Eminson   I.S.16   page 37
Private L Pocock   I.V.17   page 47
Private J Prentice   I.W.4   page 49

Bertrancourt Military Cemetery
Lance Serjeant JK Bang   I.F.12   page 65

Blighty Valley Cemetery, Authuille Wood
Serjeant JS Hepworth   I.G.11   page 81
Lance Corporal A Hill   I.A.17   page 13
Captain BD Paull   I.G.9   page 92
Private W Roberts   I.G.16   page 93
Private T Stapleton   III.C.5   page 20
Lieutenant GG Steven   I.H.11   page 112
Serjeant JH Wells   Sp.Mem. 25   page 25

Caterpillar Valley Cemetery, Longueval
Private JD Campbell   VI.D.24   page 52

Combles Communal Cemetery Extension
Lieutenant AS Carey   II.F.47   page 69
Corporal DH Noding   II.H.7   page 67
Corporal GE Pattinson   VII.A.21   page 68

Connaught Cemetery, Thiepval
Private R Fowler   I.C.23   page 12

Contay British Cemetery, Contay
Private TR Davies   IV.C.15   page 108
Lance Corporal SJA Sawyers   I.B.12   page 62
Lieutenant D'A R Wadsworth   II.A.22   page 107

Corbie Communal Cemetery Extension
Major W la T Congreve VC   I.F.35   page 36

Couin British Cemetery
Captain BH Radford   II.C.15   page 48

Danzig Alley British Cemetery, Mametz
Private A Lappin   VIII.T.1   page 14
Second Lieutenant HH Linzell   II.H.2   page 24
Private RAL Purves   I.A.53   page 53

Dartmoor Cemetery, Becordel-Becourt
Lieutenant AS Lloyd   I.C.67   page 40

Delville Wood Cemetery, Longueval
Corporal PC Buffin   IX.K.3   page 50
Serjeant WE Holt   IV.G.3   page 66
Private J Rathband   XXI.B.2   page 64

Devonshire Cemetery, Mametz
Second Lieutenant CH Shepard   B6   page 16

Dive Copse British Cemetery, Sailly-le-Sec
Rifleman S Gunn   II.C.31   page 39
Driver H Macmillan   II.A.8   page 31
Private JH Rayner   II.B.11   page 33
Second Lieutenant AT Wales   II.B.15   page 34

Douchy-les-Ayettes British Cemetery
Captain GO Roos   III.D.10   page 18

Doullens Communal Cemetery Extension No. 1
Private HA Cockerton   IV.F.15   page 94

Euston Road Cemetery, Colincamps
Serjeant JW Streets   Sp.Mem. A6   page 21

Flatiron Copse Cemetery, Mametz
Corporal E Dwyer, VC   III.J.3   page 60

Fricourt New Military Cemetery
Lieutenant AV Ratcliffe   C.8   page 15

Gommecourt British Cemetery No. 2, Hebuterne
Captain RL Hoare   IC.1   page 11
Lance Corporal CE Soper   III.F.19   page 19

Grove Town Cemetery, Meaulte
Second Lieutenant FS Chesterton   I.A.3   page 115
Serjeant L Coulson   I.J.24   page 101
Second Lieutenant TW Honychurch   I.H.5   page 86
Private F Hitchin   I.H.12   page 82
Second Lieutenant S Knowles   I.B.11   page 111

Guards' Cemetery, Lesboeufs
Second Lieutenant RF Bath   IX.V.9   page 98
Lieutenant DO Constable   VIII.N.8   page 89
Private C Doyle   XIII.R.8   page 87
Captain OA Herd   XII.K.9   page 88
Private JD Macpherson   XIII.F.8   page 76
Serjeant A Martin   VIII.D.4   page 110
Second Lieutenant R Ross   X.N.6   page 90
Lieutenant SM Scott   Sp. Mem. 33   page 72
Private WS Springett   II.Y.7   page 96
Lieutenant DP Starr   Sp.Mem.   page 74
Captain M Tennant   VIII.C.10   page 80
Guardsman WJ Williams   V.I.5   page 77

Guillemont Road Cemetery, Guillemont
Lieutenant R Asquith   I.B.3   page 70
Second Lieutenant WAS Forbes   I.A.1   page 58
Lieutenant the Hon EW Tennant   I.B.18   page 83

Heilly Station Cemetery, Mericourt-L'Abbe
Lieutenant GL Davidson · I.E.12 · page 27
Captain JENP Denning · IV.G.31 · page 91
Second Lieutenant JD Hodding · I.E.11 · page 26
Lieutenant RR Lewer · I.E.19 · page 38

Hersin Communal Cemetery Extension
Serjeant FA Hawes · I.C.4 · page 28

Hunter's Cemetery, Beaumont-Hamel
Private Donald McCallum · 19 · page 120

La Neuville Communal Cemetery, Corbie
Private Peter McLaughlan · B.14 · page 126

London Cemetery and Extension, Longueval
Captain D Henderson · 1A.A.14 · page 73
Private J Paul · 3.F.29 · page 35
Private A Tod · 2.J.3 · page 30

Lonsdale Cemetery, Authuille
Lieutenant AR Bradford · IX.A.5 · page 104
Lieutenant EE Polack · X.G.9 · page 32

Mailly Wood Cemetery, Mailly-Maillet
Lance Corporal A Ferguson · I.E.19 · page 122

Meaulte Military Cemetery
Second Lieutenant HA Butters · E.27 · page 56

Mill Road Cemetery, Thiepval
Private L Brick · I.E.19 · page 57
Lieutenant HW Hitchcock · II.B.10 · page 118
Captain A McLintock · XII.C.2 · page 61

Puchevillers British Cemetery
Private H Benzley · I.G.69 · page 44
Private WO Craib · II.D.14 · page 45
Captain M Goodall · I.B.55 · page 29
Lieutenant FA Ralfs · I.D.57 · page 79
Private LN Shepherd · II.E.4 · page 46

Ribemont Communal Cemetery Extension, Somme
Driver TG Hamilton   III.K.5   page 95

Serre Road Cemetery No. 2, Serre
Serjeant A Bath   XXIV.H.14   page 41

Varennes Military Cemetery
Brigadier General P Howell   I.B.37   page 97

Villers Station Cemetery, Villers-au-Bois
Private JT Jardine   II.B.18   page 116

Warlencourt British Cemetery
Lieutenant GJH Ashwin   I.B.11   page 114
Private JF Buckland   IV.C.10   page 123
Private EG Dornbusch   II.E.27   page 124
Private CF Hodges   III.B.11   page 125
Second Lieutenant GBT Jardine   VII.C.34   page 105
Private TJ Reynard   I.G.11   page 106
Private FW Trotman   VI.J.8   page 100

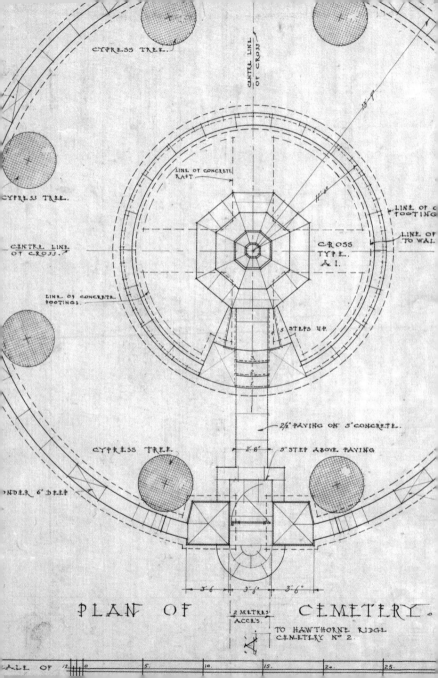

CYPRESS TREE.

CENTRE LINE OF CROSS

CYPRESS TREE.

LINE OF CONCRETE RAFT

CENTRE LINE OF CROSS.

CROSS TYPE. A.1.

LINE OF CONCRETE FOOTINGS.

LINE OF C FOOTING

LINE OF TO WAL

5 STEPS UP.

2½" PAVING ON 5" CONCRETE.

CYPRESS TREE.

2'-8'   5" STEP ABOVE PAVING

UNDER 6" DEEP

3'-6'   3'-6'   3'-6'

PLAN OF CEMETERY.

2 METRES ACCESS

'A'.

TO HAWTHORNE RIDGE CEMETERY Nº 2.

SCALE OF   12   0   5.   10.   15.   20.   25.